PARIS
HOTEL STORIES

© 2003 Assouline Publishing
601 West 26th Street, 18th Floor
New York, NY 10001 USA
Tel.: 212 989-6810 Fax: 212 647-0005
www.assouline.com

Translated and adapted from the French by David Wharry

ISBN : 2 84323 368 2

Color separation: Gravor (Switzerland)
Printing by Grafiche Milani (Italy)

TEXTS BY FRANCOIS SIMON
PHOTOGRAPHS BY DANIEL ARON

PARIS
HOTEL STORIES

ASSOULINE

Contents

Park Hyatt Paris Vendôme, *The new kid on the block*   8

Costes, *Still in the lap of fashion*   16

Ritz, *The immaculate conception*   25

Meurice, *Falsely discreet but genuinely unique*   34

Normandy, *Brighten yourself up, dust yourself off*   46

Regina, *The ineffable lightness of being*   54

Westminster, *In good hands*   64

Pavillon de la Reine, *The not-in-a-hotel experience*   74

Pershing Hall, *Between method and madness*   84

Plaza Athénée, *Tyranny of excellence*   92

Bristol, *The silent hotel*   104

George V, *A new season, a new reign*   112

Crillon, *Living a little*   120

Lancaster, *Time regained*   130

La Trémoille, *Brand new body, same old soul*   140

Concorde Saint-Lazare, *The return of a grande dame*   150

Raphaël, *The hotel on the hill*   158

Saint-James Paris, *Far from the madding crowd*   168

Square, *The egoistic pleasure of the atypical*   176

Hôtel, *The incredible invisible hotel*   186

Bel-Ami, *That friend of yours in Saint-Germain-des-Prés*   195

Villa Saint-Germain, *After the storm*   200

Lutetia, *The hotel stratosphere*   208

Montalembert, *In search of future times*   216

Villa Royale, *The crimson lady*   228

Index   236

Photos credits and acknowledgments   240

Introduction

"Paris, the only civilized city, the only place where one also finds forgiveness for the errors of one's ways and passionate admiration for every strength."

OSCAR WILDE

"All the world's a stage, and all the men and women merely players," and the great hotels know only too well that they are theaters for life's sublime ephemerality. Like the great dramatists, their role is to render life more beautiful, more intense, more passionate and exquisite. Today's globetrotters know that the moment they enter a Paris palace lobby they become the star. The hotel's task is simple: to ensure one is constantly center stage, cocooned in one's own personal limelight.

No need to learn any lines, one merely has to play oneself (or so one thinks: one is in fact being subtly cued). The hotel's mission is an exalted one, and this is why even the greatest can sometimes paint themselves into a corner. The higher the standards, the more rigorous the excellence, the more rarefied the air one creates for oneself. The purpose of such perfection is to transform the mundane affair of life into a series of delectable, indelibly etched instants.

The other role of the great hotels – and the Paris palaces are no exception – is to provide the ideal base from which to explore a city. The hotel is at the heart of the action yet must remain in the wings. Outside its padded capsule, the City of Lights awaits like a gigantic stage set, beckoning invitingly. But to enjoy it to the full one needs a friend, a confidant, an accomplice, a lover. We all need someone we can rely on, we all need to feel desired. The hotel has to know how to be all of this and more.

François Simon

"In mid-August,
one delicately colored Monday evening
A Monday floating like a feather
In Paris as bright as a new-laid egg."
PAUL ELUARD,
"PARIS DARING TO CROW OVER ITS VICTORY," 1942

PARK HYATT
PARIS VENDÔME

The new kid on the block

You dive into the Hyatt like Esther Williams, wide-eyed, bubbles fizzing through your mother-of-pearl teeth, as you enter into a fresh, raw, squeaky clean world. Yes, there is nothing quite like a brand spanking new hotel, like being welcomed by new staff wearing factory-fresh smiles and uniforms. The pile of the carpet has that virgin-territory feel underfoot as you are ushered through a muffled maze of cozy, beckoning lounge spaces. Before you know it there you are in the restaurant. You feel like you've been transported there, like a suit on a coat hanger.

The restaurant's rotunda plan and subtle layout is not bad at all. In fact, it's a relief to see a Paris palace restaurant freed from the pomp and circumstance stranglehold of the official designers (Pierre-Yves Rochon, Jacques Garcia). Another refreshing feature is the kitchen. Like the Hong Kong Hyatt and the New York Grill in Tokyo before it, the kitchen has been brought out of the wings and onto the stage. In their superb chrome décor, amidst swirling silver vapor effects, a cast of actors swathed in white play out their respective roles. And again it strikes you that this is what is so formidable about the new generation of techno-chic restaurants: the awesome deployment of energy, quality and care. It is as if they had only to press a hidden button and presto there you would be in a Michelin two-star restaurant. Because, honestly, the large Loctudy lobster with its tomato "kassoundi" and spicy salad could

easily grace the table of a three-star establishment on the Champ-Elysées. Dazzling. The turbot perfumed with bay is less "brilliant," albeit beyond reproach. And the desserts? The milk chocolate "cylinder" is a creation of the mind rather than the senses, an interesting concept but frankly a bit hard to swallow. We are in a new era here, one in which the technology of modern gastronomy has been made into a stage show, in which the kitchen has become the star.

The Park Hyatt gate-crashed its way into the Paris hotel elite, like a hit single going straight to the top ten. Which takes nerve, to say the least. The advantage in this, though, is that you bypass the extremely rigorous French star-rating certification, and therefore any price restraints. The disadvantage is you're confronting a capricious market head on. But nobody bursts into the Paris big time like this alone. The Park Hyatt Paris has the experience of a worldwide organization behind it, a 204-strong chain of hotels in 53 countries, 84,000 employees, 87,000 rooms. It all started in the middle of the night in Los Angeles in 1957, when the chain's founder, Jay Pritzker, then a humble traveling salesman and fed up with standard second-rate service in the average hotel, stumbled at last on a friendly welcome, on a hotel with good vibrations – and decided to channel all his energy into recreating this seminal experience.

Energy is the key word here, the kind of energy it takes to move mountains, the kind needed to raise by one meter the classified facades of the five period buildings acquired for the project, in a quarter whose architectural heritage is as protected as nearby Place Vendôme. But when faced with that kind of determination, the waters spontaneously part, things fall into place. The architect Ed Tuttle put the Haussmann style's classic components into a blender and out popped the Park Hyatt Paris Vendôme's keynote textures: mahogany, Paris stone, gold leaf and gilded bronze. The rooms, with their flexible, modular system of private, intimate spaces separated by sliding wooden panels, explore a different register. This Japanese concept is present in the bathrooms too, which have a large bath and a shower that can open directly into the room using the same sliding panel system. The sculptor Roseline Granet's slender bronze forms are almost obsessively omnipresent – door handles, candelabras, wall lights. But as the hotel brochure explains, they add "a unique touch of poetry to the very refined style of the rooms and suites."

The Park Hyatt has the winged grace of the debutante, the disarming candor of the new kid on the block. But she needs time to settle down. The body has arrived but hasn't had time to unpack its soul yet. And what a body. The bar, for instance: black silk wall seats, Ed Paschke's very colorful paintings, and a bartender presiding over some 70 whiskies, 20 champagnes, vintage English gins and a 1904 Tesserand cognac. Not forgetting the various lounges (between you and me, these are the ideal places to have lunch).

There will be the obligatory getting-to-know-you phase, those first rounds of mutual observation, but deep down you already know: the Hyatt is in town to stay. And in the unlikelihood that the Hyatt needed any reassurance of this, if it believed in telltale omens, then it had one right at the start. One of its very first guests, a man from the Far East, decided to get up at the crack of dawn. He set his alarm clock accordingly and slept like a baby – only to wake up in the middle of the next morning, sunbeams playing over the vast duvet of his king-size bed. This had never happened to him before. He checked his alarm clock, and laughed out loud when he realized his (subconsciously deliberate?) mistake: it was set for the right time, the right day... the following year.

à deux pas…

- *Eating around:*

the hotel has taken the food side of things very seriously. The restaurant, therefore, is more than respectable. However, it is definitely in the quieter and calmer bar and salon de thé that the choicest gourmet moments are to be had. But the Hyatt is in excellent company: on the same pavement, you have Le Céladon at the Westminster *see page 67*. And of course there is also L'Espadon at the Ritz *see page 26*. But a little further west you have two more class acts: Alain Dutournier's Carré des Feuillants *14 rue de Castiglione, 01.42.86.82.82* and, opposite, the restaurant at Hôtel Lotti, which is "advised" by the famous Milanese chef Gualtiero Marchesi *9 rue de Castiglione, 01.42.60.40.62*. Also recommended is the Italian restaurant at Hôtel Cortile *37 rue Cambon, 01.44.58.45.67*. Parisian brasserie lovers should make straight for Flottes *2 rue Cambon, 01.42.60.80.89*.

- *Shopping around:*

Cartier, Dunhill, Lancel, Ermenegildo Zegna, Tiffany's: the top designers and brands await you with open arms. Galerie Vivienne is also well worth a visit *entry on rue des Petits-Champs*. The shoe connoisseurs can go to 2 rue de la Paix, at Massaro, to order made-to-measure items.

- *Brain food:*

Opéra comique *5 rue Favart, 01.42.44.45.45*, théâtre du Palais-Royal *38 rue Montpensier, 01.42.97.59.81*, Comédie-Française *1 place Colette, 01.44.58.15.15*, musée Grévin *10 bd Montmartre, 01.47.70.85.05*… just choose!

- *Hair stylist:*

the color specialist, Rodolphe at Coloré *26 rue Danielle-Casanova* is only two minutes away.

- *Breakfast:*

for strong Lavazza coffee, La Colombe opposite the hotel. Press junkies must go either to place du Marché-Saint-Honoré or, from 10 a.m., Brentano's Franco-American bookshop *37 avenue de l'Opéra*.

PARK HYATT

3-5 RUE DE LA PAIX 75002 PARIS

TEL.: +33 (1) 58 71 12 34
FAX: +33 (1) 58 71 12 35

E-MAIL RESERVATIONS:
vendome@paris.hyatt.com
Website: www.paris.vendome.hyatt.com

- *Double rooms from 600 dollars,*
  suites from 800 dollars,
  159 rooms and 29 suites
- *Le Park restaurant*
- *Health spa with sauna*
- *Hammam and gym*

Transparency
The Park Hyatt Vendôme is the latest in the Hyatt chain to open up its kitchens and turn the cooking of your meal into a "live show."

Multiple choice
One of the Park Hyatt's strengths is undoubtedly the way it modulates its cuisine, from haute gastronomie served here in the hotel's flagship restaurant to the less elaborate dishes served in the lounges.

Around midnight
A highlight of any jazz number is often its solo improvisation and the same goes for a hotel's bar, which can range from the timid and reserved to the lively and expressive, like the Park Hyatt's here.

Space
You may well feel like lingering in the hotel's warm, airy public spaces, a symphony of Paris stone, mahogany, gold leaf and gilded bronze.

COSTES

Still in the lap of fashion

Paris's latest cult hotel was a love child, and here she is almost ten years later, still in the lap of fashion, not yet in her teens but already the stuff that dreams are made of. And already with so many stories to tell, tales in which fact and fiction often mingle, a world in which the novels and short stories that have been set here rub shoulders with the real-life romances. Newspaper legend has it that Vanessa Paradis and Johnny Depp first set eyes on each other here – the rest is already history. And the Costes cast list can indeed often be as deliciously improbable as a novel's. Today, the actor Jamel Debbouze and a crowned head of Spain are both demanding the same room. Soccer goalie Fabien Barthez is arriving shortly. Meanwhile, an achingly beautiful guest artist makes her Costes début, her stiletto heels half-disappearing into the purple lobby carpet with each step.

A decade ago Hôtel Costes was the down-at-the-heels Hôtel de France et de Choiseul. Nicknamed the "petit Bristol," it had known better times but still kept a certain coarse charm. (One relishes the idea of some unsuspecting tour operator, unaware of the change in management several years ago, disgorging a coach of senior citizens outside the hotel today.) The hotel had undeniable potential, with its courtyard garden and 120 rooms. Jean-Louis Costes and his brother Gilbert left their native town of Aveyron in southern France to seek their fortunes in the capital. And, as is her habit, Lady Luck smiled on the brave and the bold, especially those not afraid of hard work. One only has to meet the Costes brothers, though, to realize where their true strength lies: in those eyes, watching you, studying you. Jean-Louis Costes entered the world of luxury hotels as a cook. In the kitchens of the Plaza he first took the hotel business's pulse, and he understood that luxury

lies in the detail, in the minutest gestures of a performance and mise en scène, in the sublimation of the simple.

As in every great theatrical production, therefore, the set design was crucial: the elongated, introspective overture of the lobby; the narrow, circular, catwalk of a corridor; the multiple tables echoing the spectacle. Jean-Louis Costes understood that a whole new generation of golden boys and girls was aspiring to a luxury that was efficient without being (too) ostentatious, one that knew how to be sexy, pleasant and courteous yet didn't take itself too seriously. Away with the millstone of tradition, no more marble mausoleums, gone the monogrammed boredom of interminable dinners.

Yet it was precisely on the dinner plate that the Costes theme took form. The hotel's kitchens saw the genesis of an astonishing gastronomy, a light, almost playful cuisine composed of couldn't-be-simpler dishes inspired by... why, the great palaces, of course. "Snacks" for the amusement of both palate and tongue: Costes' menus, with their linguistic pirouettes and puns, are gems of minimalist literature. Words, gently held between their tonglike inverted commas, leave the page to become impishly mischievous dishes on your plate. A poetry that initially drew groans but to whose modernist simplicity, it seems, people have now grown accustomed. Costes, in the spirit of the time, purposefully sets out to be flighty and superficial yet with all the verve of the carefree and spirited. At Costes you don't eat – you take sustenance, you peck at your food and, like a child, stop when no longer hungry. Costes appetites are meager, intense, kept rigorously in check.

The menu often proceeds like a model on the catwalk, in a succession of postures, freezing for the photographers between strides and twirls, teasing you with tongue-in-cheek sound bites like "minute browned," "mildly spicy" or "enough for two"– an ironic poetry sublimating futility, taking nothing seriously, taunting, stinging with wasplike lucidity. The service, too, is a deliciously glamorous affair. Costes waiters and waitresses have outgrown their traditional walk-on roles and become little fleeting divas. And you, the client, obediently enter into a server-served role reversal, only too pleased to play the well-behaved, patient slave of these attentive master and mistress figures. You do so willingly, knowing full well that it is precisely in this kind of game that the Costes spirit expresses itself most completely. You find yourself swept into the hotel's passion for detail, drawn in by every supreme little extra effort it makes for you. The bath curtains,

for instance, are cotton. "Presumably, they're changed for each new client?"
The reply is a wounded look.

The design of the rooms is by Jacques Garcia, whose decor of stripes, purples and famous red lampshades (the most copied accessory in Paris) achieve a boudoir atmosphere steeped in luxury. "I've often been criticized about the red," he says, amused. "Yet it's a color that can put problematic spaces right. I don't set out to annoy, I'm friendly by nature." What strikes one in Hôtel Costes is its half light, its shadows – it's as if one were wearing sunglasses. Jean-Louis Costes explains, "I wanted people who stay here to find real rest, that indispensable break. The lifestyle of our clients is often frenetic. Spotlights and flashbulbs are constantly trained on them. When night comes they want to get away from all that. This is why the lights are low and a plug for the computer is frankly not de rigueur." In fact, the hotel foils its defects (the absence of view and its hemmed-in aspect) by playing on them. Recently, when more windows onto the street became available, they were immediately painted black. The chic that Costes exudes is a blend of strangeness, charm, sophistication and the nonchalance of the new century's spoiled children: carefully unconsidered.

à deux pas…

- *Those wishing to remain on planet Costes:*
merely have to pop over for breakfast, brunch or "le Five O'clock" at Marly, in the courtyard of the Louvre *Cour Napoléon, 93 rue de Rivoli; 01.49.26.06.60* or to the more trendy Café Ruc *159 rue Saint-Honoré, 01.42.60.97.54.* Further afield, on the outer reaches of the Costes orbit, are Etienne Marcel *34 rue Etienne-Marcel, 01.45.08.01.03* and Georges *top floor and terrace of the Pompidou Center, 01.44.78.47.99,* whose breathtaking view out over the city more than compensates for the less than cutting edge cuisine.

- *Retail therapy:*
for fashion, design, gadgets and beauty product junkies, Colette *21 rue Saint-Honoré,* obviously, and then, to prevent your credit card from catching fire, the Water Bar downstairs or the store's new offbeat superette. And don't forget Chanel and the tailor-made corset shop, Alice Cadolle, on rue Cambon.

- *Sustenance:*
you don't even have to leave the hotel, since in-house you have one of Paris's trendiest eating places, but those hankering after a few extra calories can always defect to Lyonnais *32 rue Saint-Marc, 01.42.96.65.04,* Alain Ducasse's latest creation in collaboration with Thierry de la Brosse of l'Ami Louis *32 rue du Vertbois, 01.48.87.77.48,* another fashionable address.

- *Fashion:*
Maria Luisa: the women's boutique is at *2 rue Cambon,* the men's store at *19bis rue du Mont-Thabor,* the unisex shop is at *38 rue du Mont-Thabor* and the accessories are at *4 rue Cambon.*

- *Hair:*
John Nollet *32 rue Montorgueil, 01.55.80.71.50.* A movie specialist: Audrey Tautou, Monica Bellucci, Virginie Ledoyen, to name but a few.

- *Croissants and press:*
the Blason at 233 rue Saint-Honoré.

COSTES

239 RUE SAINT-HONORÉ 75001 PARIS

TEL: +33 (1) 42 44 50 00
FAX: +33 (1) 42 44 50 01

RESERVATIONS ONLY BY PHONE

- *Double rooms from 315 to 650 dollars, suites from 725 to 3500 dollars, 79 rooms, 3 suites*
- *Restaurant •*
Swimming-pool • Hammam
- *Fitness club*

Outside
The hotel's courtyard restaurant is the place to be seen in Paris. The city's In Crowd flock there every day of the week to gauge their fame rating in peer-group surroundings.

Inside
But at Costes the most delectable action takes place in the small lounges indoors. The most sought-after tables are around the fireplace, where one is elegantly but not always that comfortably seated.

Sleep
Costes sleep is deep and warm, like black velvet. The decor, between baroque and boudoir, slows the night down, draws it out, with the lights kept soothingly low for flash-weary trendsetters.

The next morning
Take the lift down to the most trendy fitness club in Paris, take a dip in the pool and enjoy the hammam and fellow beautiful people before returning to the fray of the city.

RITZ

The immaculate conception

Standing in Place Vendôme gazing at the hallowed facade, you wonder by what miracle such a hotel came into being. You suspect the answer is beyond the comprehension of mortals, cloaked in myth. Phrases like "And then there was the Ritz," or "On the eighth day God created the Ritz" come to mind. Or did one of the most revered hotels in the world just magically spring from the ground one day? You watch two maids at a window ritualistically maneuvering a set of the three-meter-high louvered shutters shut. The American couple who arrived this morning are about to sleep off some of their jetlag. For the maids, beginning the afternoon shift, the day has hardly begun. The Ritz has the highest staff-guest ratio in Paris (600 for 133 rooms and 42 suites). The woman in command of this army, the head housekeeper, Mlle. Metrot, is one of the Paris hotel world's living legends. Daily, she scours the Ritz for the slightest defect. Nothing escapes her eye, a weak light bulb here, the wrinkles in a brocaded Venice silk velvet cushion there, the scuff on the armchair over there... In her wake, her retinue of craftsmen leap into action, pots of the famous Ritz pinkish-beige (reference number 0103B) and gold paint at the ready. Nothing is overlooked. Even the bathroom towels are inspected to see whether their color tints match exactly – unlike the rank and file of Paris palaces, the Ritz owns its linen (cream with a caramel motif), and the hotel laundry staff is responsible for grading items into different color "vintages."

A royal delegation passes in the corridor. Head respectfully lowered, you watch the reflection of the Queen of Thailand pass in the gleaming brass ball at the end of the banister rail. From the window you watch the perfectly choreographed scene outside as she gets into her car amidst the paranoid quickstep and shuffle of bodyguards. The Queen has taken over

part of the hotel; three rooms have been converted into kitchens for her. And no doubt her major-domos have long ago mastered the Ritz's ornate leaf-patterned light switches – many an exasperated Ritz novice has phoned reception for the secret. "Monsieur, one simply has to give a little turn, like this. Voilà."

On planet Ritz everyone dreams the same dreams: of staying in the Chanel suite (whose musky fragrance remains a mystery – the Chinese fabrics?), or the Elton John (432–433), or 629–630 (John F. Kennedy, Jr.'s, with its view out over the Paris Opéra). But there are those who prefer the Cambon wing where, one devotee confides, "You can scream your head off if you want." And of course there is the restaurant, L'Espadon, where the Ritz guest is put in his rightful place, that of king – if only an ephemeral one. There was a time when L'Espadon, like other Paris palace restaurants, cultivated an exquisitely dated quality. The result was an impression of a world on the wane, of an excellence a bit short of breath, no longer frankly so very excellent. And there were of course the patrons that went with it: the greatest concentration of haughty self-assurance one was ever likely to set eyes on. Faces just asking to be smacked. Where did they think they were, at the Ritz? A bygone age, thankfully, since all has now changed. While many of its Paris peers have been content to wallow in their culinary

self-satisfaction, the Ritz has moved on, stepped up the pace. Without throwing everything —caviar, lobster and all that— to the wind, of course, merely letting in fresh breezes from elsewhere. Crab in citrus juice, filet mignon with onion chutney, bass à la citronella... But if comeback there has been then it is also due to a whole new service credo at L'Espadon. Enter a new breed of waiters content merely to do their job, who take away plates or inquire as to one's wishes when necessary, who disappear and reappear when required, who, in short, keep out of your way. There are delicious ritzy instants when one could almost imagine oneself in a James Bond movie, or at Maxim's during la Belle Epoque, mischievous little miracles of Paris palace kitsch that are there to be savored, at least once. The prices are vertiginous, admittedly, but there honestly isn't anything to stop you from skipping the starter if you want – like true gentlemen, no Ritz waiter would ever let a frown of disapproval furrow his brow.

And in the Hemingway Bar you can play at being a master of the universe or whomever you wish as long as you say "please." For here, for better or for worse, you will be in the capable hands of Colin P. Field, who, if you so desire, is capable of the very best and worst (matching the color of your cocktail to the color of your tie, for instance). Whatever you do, don't leave this man in peace. Monsieur Field is a mine of wisdom and information and a

model of charm and discretion, especially with those he doesn't (yet) know.

"Monsieur would like?"

"White wine—sizzling cold."

"Bien, monsieur."

A twirl of the torso, a bottle is resurrected from a freezer vault, sub-zero nectar is eased into a tall tulip glass. We talk about Hemingway (who demanded his white wine be served like that) and the man's oddball tastes in libation: he liked his mojitos and daiquiris with lots of ice and his double whiskies topped with frozen water. The conversation shifts to a certain Parisian bar (Harry's Bar) and its tenuous claim to the paternity of the Bloody Mary and the sidecar. Colin P. Field's ritzy stoicism becomes solemn indignation. He says, "I'm not interested in legends, only the truth." The bar's clientele varies with the time of day, from those who come to savor the languorous peace of the 6:30 to 7:30 slot to the exquisite mix of the 10:30-to-midnight congregation, an invariably sublime cocktail of various shades of wealth, fame, fortune and beauty. Shaken not stirred.

à deux pas…

- *Take-home Paris:*
once you've done the rounds of the Place Vendôme and rue de la Paix jewelers, don't forget Goyard, the famous luggage maker *233 rue Saint-Honoré.* For beauty products of the same ilk, Stéphane Marais *217 rue Saint-Honoré.* On your way there, one of the rare Guerlain stores in Paris *on the corner of Saint-Honoré and Castiglione.*

- *Bistrot parisien:*
the most authentic is incontestably the Petit Vendôme *8 rue des Capucines, 01.42.61.05.88,* with its sandwiches and plats du jour and guaranteed cocky Parisian attitude.

- *Lingerie:*
for a boudoir style somewhere between Betty Boop and Marylin Monroe, Fifi Chachnil *26 rue Cambon, 01.42.60.38.86.*

- *Lunch en tête à tête:*
the Duke's Bar at the Hôtel Westminster *13 rue Daunou, 01.42.61.57.46.*

- *Wee small hours:*
no need for room service, the night is still young at Chez Denise *5 rue des Prouvaires, 01.42.36.21.82:* pot au feu or côte de bœuf for two and the company of fellow ravenous night owls like you.

- *A brand new day:*
at Angelina *226 rue de Rivoli.*

RITZ PARIS

15 PLACE VENDÔME 75001 PARIS

TEL.: +33 (1) 43 16 30 30
FAX: +33 (1) 43 16 36 68/69

E-MAIL RESERVATIONS:
resa@ritzparis.com
Website: www.ritzparis.com

• Double rooms from 620 to 800 dollars, suites from 875 to 8000 dollars, 107 rooms and 55 suites • Espadon restaurant • Ritz Escoffier School (French cuisine School) • Two bars • 7 reception rooms • 24-hour room service • Health spa (massage, sauna, hammam, swimming pool, squash) • Beauty salon

Underworld

Invent any pretext (you'd like to visit the cooking school, for example) to go downstairs and experience the myriad wonders of the Ritz's subterranean city of cooks and craftsmen.

Children

A palace often reserves its most thoughtful touches for the intimacy of its rooms—teddy bears for its youngest guests, for instance.

Regal

One of the incessant delights of the Ritz is its extraordinary variety of spaces: the interminable corridor leading to the Hemingway Bar, its gardens and lounges or, here, a staircase winding regally upwards to the rooms.

Dip

No stay at the Ritz could ever be complete without a visit to one of the hotel's most exquisitely peaceful places, the Ritz Health Club. Take a dip in the divine swimming pool and try the gym and health spa.

MEURICE

———— •◆• ————

Falsely discreet but genuinely unique

When the Meurice closed on March 18, 1999, it was as if a book had been shut with no certainty it could ever be reopened. A reopening was promised, of course, with increased comfort, more basements, more electric cables, more everything, but nothing could alleviate the sadness at seeing history dismantled like this. Each time one passed the old lady, eviscerated, shrouded in dustsheets, one mourned. It took almost two years to rebuild her. But when the bandages were taken off the post-facelift Meurice, instead of merely heaving a huge sigh of relief, Parisians gasped with surprise. The old lady looked a hundred years younger! A long-forgotten Meurice that had disappeared in the mists of time had been restored to its original splendor. Take the winter garden, for instance. When the hotel was renovated in 1905, a study was made of the natural light inside. A huge skylight roof was erected over the Four Seasons Room, its glass engraved with fish-scale motifs. With time, the cast-iron supporting structure rusted and was replaced by glass bricks set in metal and concrete. Later, in the sixties, the room's natural lighting disappeared behind a false ceiling, on which the starry heavens were painted as a consolation. But now the original winter garden is back, complete with its fish-scale roof and friezes, bathed in daylight anew.

Curiously, though, the Maurice, which rightly prides itself on its great privacy, is above all a hotel for the extravagant, for those in search of intense, exquisite moments. And also a hotel with episodes in its past that it would prefer to brush under the carpet.

In 1940 General Dietrich von Choltitz, the Nazi military commander of Paris, chose the Meurice as his headquarters and remained there throughout World War II. Yet we are indebted to the general. He immediately fell in love with the city and courageously chose to disregard his orders to destroy Paris's principal monuments. It was von Choltitz himself who signed the German surrender in the first-floor lounge. Some of the Meurice's most illustrious guests have stayed on the same floor: royals such as the Prince of Wales, the Shah of Persia and the Bey of Tunis were regular guests. King Alfonso XIII of Spain used

to bring his own furniture with him from Madrid.

And Salvador Dalí always insisted on staying in Alfonso's rooms. For more than thirty years, he lived in the formal royal suite (today 106–108). The painter wiped his brushes on the walls, and his pet leopards sharpened their claws on the carpets. But one of his greatest delights was knowing that when he went to the toilet he was sitting on the same seat as the king of Spain. One day, when he discovered that the wooden seat had been replaced by a plastic one, he roared, "What have you done with the royal throne of King

Alfonso XIII?" The hotel was ransacked in search of the relic, it was found and Dalí subsequently hung it on a wall in his villa at Cadaques. The director has an endless supply of Dalí anecdotes. The cocktail parties he organized, for instance, which he didn't attend until, when everyone had arrived, he burst in and bombarded everyone with custard tarts. Or the time he asked for a herd of goats to be driven up to his room. When they arrived in the corridor, he started firing at them with his pistol. But the bullets were blanks. Another time it was a horse. And then of course there were the flies. He paid the Meurice staff to go out into the Tuileries gardens to catch them, 5 francs a fly. And would you like to know the secret of his splendid moustache (divulged by a member of the Meurice's hair salon staff, which closed in 1974)? Before smoothing it into shape, he dipped it in fig jam.

But palace reputations are not built on anecdote alone. One of the pillars of the Meurice's renown is its restaurant, with its classical French cuisine and impressive marble pilasters, which gives onto the Tuileries gardens. And one other thing about the restaurant: one of the bronze and crystal chandeliers belongs to yours truly. After I won a bet on the year of a bottle of wine, the director at the time, circumspect about my beginner's luck but a good loser all the same, decided to give it to me.

But the true power of the new Meurice lies in its rooms. Formerly 180 in number, now 160, they have been totally reinvented, given thicker, more soundproof skins and immaculate marble bathrooms (some are in the red and ochre Pyrenees marble used at Versailles). The first floor, with its presidential suites, has kept its official air, but the higher one goes the more Parisian the decor becomes. On the sixth floor —in 604 and 605, for example— the dormer windows give the rooms a more intimate feel. We walk quietly past 601, where this morning Rupert Everett is still asleep. Room 528 has its regulars too. For some reason the room is a favorite of fashion editors – single fashion editors, the director adds, almost as an explanation. Yet the room is vast, and the wardrobe cavernous (could that be why?). The bathroom, too, is exquisite: it looks out on Montmartre and the Sacre Coeur. Then there is the seventh floor and the Belle Etoile (Under the Stars) Suite. One can easily imagine sleeping under the stars, curled up in a sleeping bag on the 250-square-meter terrace, shunning the even larger suite inside, gazing out over the Tuileries, the Eiffel Tower, the Champs-Elysées, the Arc de Triomphe... Yes, out here one understands just how unique the Meurice really is.

à deux pas…

- *Shopping around:*
along rue de Rivoli you have Galignani's English bookshop at n°. 224, *when you leave go and have tea at Angelina next door at n°. 226*. Rue Saint-Honoré is just round the corner: Hermes, Gucci, Yves Saint-Laurent, Lacroix, *et al.* are on the other side of the rue Royale intersection, in rue du Faubourg-Saint-Honoré.

- *Health matters:*
on rue Castiglione, you'll find the Pharmacy Swann *6 rue de Castiglione*: it originally belonged to Marcel Proust's uncle. Swann's present pharmacist, the remarkable and endearing Yolande Champenier di Giovani, even stocks Knizze beauty products.

- *Café, croissants, papers:*
for British and American papers go along rue de Rivoli to WH Smith's, the English bookshop at no. 248, then go and have coffee or even a meal at the delicious brasserie Flottes *2 rue Cambon, 01.42.60.80.89* – the French fries are fantastic.

- *Hunger pangs:*
there are several discreet eateries nearby including the Japanese restaurant Kinugawa *3 rue du Mont-Tabor, 01.42.60.65.07* and the Franco-Italian Il Palazzo at the Hôtel Normandy *1 rue d'Argenteuil, 01.42.60.91.20*. If you're looking for Parisian-style bistros, go a little further along rue Saint-Honoré to Le Dauphin at 167 *01.42.60.40.11* or, closer, to Lescure *7 rue de Mondovi, 01.42.60.18.91*, a restaurant whose traditional down-to-earth French cuisine, *bœuf bourguignon, confit de canard,* is popular with employees of the United States Consulate just next door.

- *One more for the road:*
Harry's New York bar is only a ten minute walk away at *5 rue Daunou* or, even better, the Hemingway Bar at the Ritz is just round the corner; and don't forget to drop in at the bar at the Meurice for that last drink.

MEURICE

228 RUE DE RIVOLI 75001 PARIS

TEL.: +33 (1) 44 58 10 10
FAX: +33 (1) 44 58 10 15

E-MAIL RESERVATIONS:
reservations@meuricehotel.com
Website: www.meuricehotel.com

- *Double rooms from 675 to 850 dollars, suites from 1300 to 1950 dollars (enquire for the large and royal suites), 125 rooms, 36 suites including two 250m² presidential suites and the 275m² "Belle Étoile" seventh-floor penthouse suite*
- *Restaurant • Bar • Reception rooms • Sauna • Beauty salon • Fitness club*

Gastronomy

Noblesse oblige, the Meurice's restaurant, like that of the other great Parisian palaces, is dedicated to French gastronomy and France's most prestigious culinary specialties—not forgetting an impressive wine list, of course.

Counterpoint

The winter garden's spectacular skylight, previously hidden above a concrete ceiling demolished during the hotel's renovation, perfectly echoes the lightness and finesse of the restaurant's cuisine.

Slow-release

The Meurice reveals its full splendor gradually, in its upper floors. The best is at the top: rooms 604, 605 and 601 (Rupert Everett's favorite) are quite simply Paris at its most exquisite.

Awesome

The Belle Etoile Suite, with its 250 square meters of terraces and a 360° view of Paris: Tuileries, Louvre, Champs Elysées, Eiffel Tower, the lot.

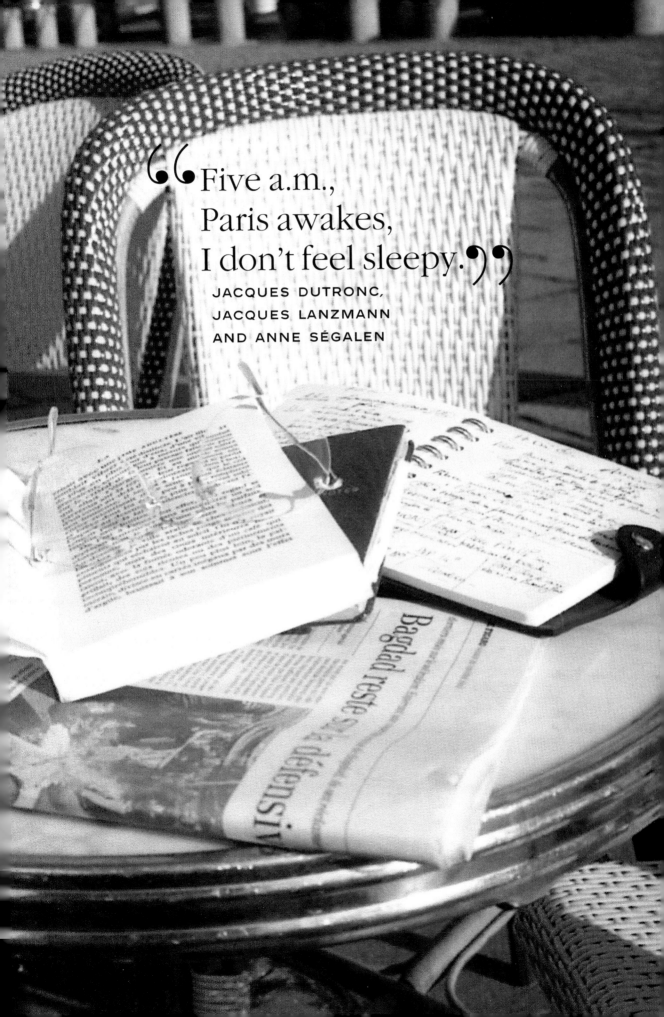

"Five a.m.,
Paris awakes,
I don't feel sleepy."
JACQUES DUTRONC,
JACQUES LANZMANN
AND ANNE SÉGALEN

NORMANDY

Brighten yourself up,
dust yourself off

There are those hotels where ghosts pull the strings, where history has the last word. Exquisitely well-mannered and polite hotels with impeccable posture, who know how to behave like a gentleman; hotels whose daily existences are as well ordered as Phineas Fogg's, whose workings are as regulated as a music box.

The Normandy is one such hotel, one of those familiar pieces of Parisian furniture, which despite its almost insolent location slap bang in the middle of it all –the Palais Royal, the Louvre, the Tuileries, rue du Faubourg Saint-Honoré– one hardly notices at all. One of those impressive Haussmann-style edifices one barely gives a second look, automatically assuming it to be full of specialist doctors' and lawyers' offices. The kind of prime real estate that is never sold, that remains in the family... until it was taken over by the Hôtels de Paris Group (25 hotels in Paris including the Villa Beaumarchais, the Villa Lutèce and the Villa Royale). A group that likes to give each of its hotels a distinct style: hunting, turn-of-the-century Montparnasse, the Moulin Rouge (the Villa Royale).

And the Normandy? Well, it can often be the guest who fashions a hotel's destiny. Nobody quite knows why a certain hotel has become the darling of the fashion world, why another is favored by antique dealers, or another by judges and lawyers. In the Normandy's case it was the Americans and English. All you need is a word (Normandy) and a style – an indefinable style encompassing the Renaissance and

Formica, which the Normandy perfectly seriously calls "modern classical" – and you have an atmosphere, an old-world feel, a very European climate of chandeliers, period furniture, old Parisian engravings and rather solemn lighting; in a word, history.

But the hotel's new owners felt they had to do something, brighten things up a bit, get things moving. And there's nothing like the pneumatic drill for wakening things up, and discovering things. A partition wall was knocked down, not to reveal a skeleton or a fifty-year-old breakfast tray behind it but a forgotten staircase, a ghostly six-story spiral of dusty steps. But this was nothing compared to what was discovered in the restaurant.

During World War II the low-ranking German officers billeted at the Normandy (the top ranks stayed at the Crillon) found the dining room too difficult to heat and built a false ceiling to halve the room's volume. Which was never taken down. And when the Hôtels de Paris pneumatic drills went to work, what did they reveal, seven meters from the floor? A magnificent ceiling covered in frescoes and gold leaf, complete with marble and cast-iron columns. The experts who were immediately summoned uttered the words the management was waiting, hoping to hear: "Even more beautiful than the ceilings in the Meurice and the Crillon."

The hotel was brightened, lightened up, given back the pride it had been gradually losing. The dining room is now almost unbelievably superb. One is literally dumbstruck. The designer Marc Dumas, a pupil of Starck, could have fallen headlong into the age-old trap, but didn't. In the modern France of "cohabitation," ancient and modern (his magnificent bell-shaped copper ceiling lights) can be perfectly complementary. Risks were successfully taken in the kitchen, too. Chef Thierry Barot's Italian cuisine revisited à la française was a hazardous venture, but it works. Crab cannelloni, bass cooked in a sea-salt crust perfumed with wild fennel, tiramusu, pistachio ice cream, amaretto... The English-style bar –where in June 1940 General de Gaulle had his last drink in Paris before leaving for Bordeaux and then London– is about to be modified as well. It was also here, in rue de l'Echelle, that a carriage pulled up during the night of June 20, 1792. A group of people furtively hurried the hundred paces from the Louvre and got inside. The coachman who immediately whipped the horses into a gallop was none other than the Comte de Fersan. His

passengers were Louis XVI, Marie Antoinette and their children. The count's mission: to take them to safety. But they had embarked on a journey that would seal their fate. They were recognized in the village of Varennes and arrested. Six months later Louis XVI was the first to be publicly beheaded.

And that's just what clients love about the Normandy: the knowledge that there are those phantoms in the wardrobes, and that the hotel has plenty more playfully kept up its sleeve.

à deux pas…

- *Shopping*:
why deprive yourself? The Palais-Royal, just across the road, has to be one of the most beautiful shopping malls in the world. In this sublime architectural setting, pay a visit to Prince Louis-Albert de Broglie's showcase store Le Prince Jardinier, the Palais-Royal salons - Shiseido, Didier Ludot…

- *Eating around*:
people come from far afield to savor the elegant Franco-Italian cuisine of the Normandy's restaurant, Il Palazzo, but there is also plenty to attract you outside. Try Le Dauphin in front of the Comédie-Française *167 rue Saint-Honoré, 01.42.60.40.11*. Homesick Scotsmen may opt for Tim Johnston's convivial wine bar *47 rue de Richelieu, 01.42.97.46.49*. And one of my favorite restaurants, the charming Restaurant du Palais-Royal, is but a stone's throw away *110 galerie de Valois, 01.40.20.00.27*. Another "very good" address is Georges *11 rue du Mail, 01.42.60.07.11*.

- *Bottle bank*:
Legrand, 1 rue de la Banque *01.42.60.07.12* remains one of Paris's finest vintners.

- *Shopping quandary*:
here you are stuck midway between Paris's two fashion Meccas, rue Saint-Honoré and Place des Victoires, wondering which way to turn… If you're tempted by the former, refer to the Meurice, Westminster, Costes and Regina pages. But if you opt for Place des Victoires, first do the rounds of the square: *Cacharel, Kenzo, Plein Sud…* then take in the host of trendy designer boutiques along rue Etienne Marcel, with the obligatory pause for lunch *or merely a vitamin juice* at the new Costes café Etienne Marcel, at *n°. 34*.

- *Skin care*:
for Hungarian cosmetics—yogurt extract, clay, vegetable oils, etc.—Patyka *14 rue Rambuteau*.

NORMANDY

7 RUE DE L'ÉCHELLE 75001 PARIS

TEL.: +33 (1) 42 60 30 21
FAX: +33 (1) 42 60 17 09

E-MAIL RESERVATIONS:
normandy@hotelsparis.fr
Website: www.hotelsparis.fr

- *Double rooms
from 280 to 350 dollars,
suites at 460 dollars,
110 rooms, 4 suites and 1 flat*
- *Il Palazzo Italian restaurant*

Stairs
This isn't the staircase discovered during the Normandy's recent renovation but the "official" staircase to the hotel's 110 rooms and 4 suites.

Moldings
The hotel is extremely ornately decorated, the cherry on the Normandy cake being the superb moldings and gold leaf on the ceiling that were recently uncovered in the Palazzo restaurant.

Corridors
The Normandy occupies several buildings, with their maze of corridors leading from one wing to the other, abruptly changing direction or level.

Bar
Soak up the atmosphere in the delectably outdated bar while you still can: The management has decided that it is due for a makeover.

REGINA

—————◆—————

The ineffable lightness of being

There are those Parisian moments one learns to draw out, whose magic, if it is to be fully savored, must be experienced in a kind of cerebral slow motion. Sublime instants that could otherwise slip by almost unheeded, drowned out by an evening's delectable solemnity, smothered by the fatigue of a journey or lost in the emotion of a long-awaited meeting. La Tour d'Argent is a case in point. You know all about the restaurant's world reputation, you're expecting the glorious panoramic view and the fabled roast duck with its own serial number, but nothing can prepare you for what awaits you when you step out of the elevator on the top floor. Slow down, let Paris's slow-spun magic cast its spell with each step... and in that suspended moment watch the restaurant stand still around you. A velvet hush descends; waiters, like an awaiting guard of honor, withdraw as you pass. A momentary, fleeting collide of eternity and subtlety has opened up; and then life resumes.

At the Regina, on the corner of rue de Rivoli and Place des Pyramides, that rare moment awaits you on the inside of the polished-oak revolving door with its curved glass panes. The door wasn't always the unique feature it is today: once upon a time before security regulations many a Paris hotel had one. If the Regina's door continues its merry-go-round today it is thanks to nearby glass doors, ready to open at the slightest security alert. That curious freeze-frame feeling again, as if you had entered a kind of slow-motion centrifuge. Is the door lazily whisking you into temporary

limbo? You wouldn't mind it; there is that willing suspension of disbelief, an inherent complicity in places like the Regina. You don't feel like pinching yourself but closing your eyes (aren't all travelers really just overgrown children?). Or could this be a scene in some imaginary movie, you're wondering? The movie of your life? Inside, a piano stands dormant, its keyboard waiting to be brought to life by a melody. The movie theme? But your movie is just one of a long line of movies already shot there – scenes from Volker Schloendorff's *Swann in Love* (1984), starring Ornella Mutti, Jeremy Irons, Alain Delon and Simone Signoret; Alain Resnais's *Same Old Song* (1997), with Lambert Wilson, André Dussollier, Sabine Azéma; Francis Girod's *La Banquière* (1980), starring Romy Schneider, Jean-Louis Trintignant and Jean-Claude Brialy.

Yours is a movie with no title, with only two actors and the most beautiful of all revolving-door openings... which leads into a long traveling shot along an entrance hall from another age. Your roving camera eye tracks past the green porcelain lamps of the reception desk, the cash desk like a polished-oak sentry box... everything bathed in the light beaming through vast cinemascope windows framing the Place des

Pyramides and the gilded statue of Joan of Arc outside. Yet two years ago those same windows and the hallowed revolving door were blown to smithereens in a terrifying shootout between drug barons; the reception desk was riddled with lead; bullet-ridden moldings and shattered chandeliers came tumbling down – but it was just another movie, *The Kiss of the Dragon* (2001), starring Bridget Fonda, Jet Li and Tchéky Karyo. And there was no need for repair work: the sacrilege was carried out in a studio reconstruction of the hotel you're walking through now.

The entrance hall orchestrates your arrival, ushers you toward the various salons, draws you effortlessly into the recently restored Rivoli salon, where you mistakenly assume the cherubs have patrolled the ceilings of this heavenly abode since time immemorial. Not at all; they were recently resurrected from purgatory in Paris's Saint-Ouen flea market and discreetly let loose in these new skies. Other salons slip into view: the tearoom with its English-style wood paneling, Persian carpets and spacious armchairs; and the restaurant, Le Pluvinel, with its superb Art Nouveau frescoes, stained glass, Majorelle fireplace in sculpted wood and large mural mosaics of the banks of the Seine and the Tuileries gardens.

Yet this discreet, stately, turn-of-the-century elegance harbors a paradox. The Regina is undoubtedly the sole Paris hotel to breathe a certain lightness into Parisian life. A kind of indolent, languid reverie reigns throughout, in the amused, tender coquetry of its honey-colored woodwork, in the delicate curlicues of its Art Nouveau decoration. One discovers different, more austere atmospheres upstairs, where the Art Nouveau is earlier, more restrained. The well-behaved seriousness of the first-floor corridors, for instance, with their green Empire-style ceramic tiling and monumental cast-iron radiators decorated with subtle floral motifs. Genuine, magnificently restored Louis XIV armchairs, like figures from another age, await you with open arms as the elevator doors part. One hardly dares sit down on a chair for fear of being drawn away into their reveries, their reminiscences. Besides, if one did, one would deprive them of their front-row view of the elevator as the doors part on the successive scenes enacted on the stage inside, brief cameos played out by unknown (but not always) actors like yourself. One could sit for hours in front of those doors opening and closing on gaiety, solitude, hope: an expectant young couple with only hand luggage, then a solitary, pre-occupied man, and so on. Caught in this oak-paneled photo booth, people of all nationalities come and go, but there is always that something extra, that strange magic, the soupçon of mystery that great hotels bestow on apparently mundane, vaguely drifting lives. Appearances can be so superbly misleading. Who was waiting for you in the wee small hours in room 133 (the one with the tiles with the tulip motif in the bathroom)? What lost dream were you tracking down in your sleep? Whose was the hand you held before leaving? Each room contains its own stage direction, its own choreography. And those views down rue de Rivoli and across the Tuileries gardens hold you spellbound for hours (rooms 9, 10, 11, 12, 15, 17, 19); not to mention the balcony rooms (first and sixth floors), and of course the suites. For instance, 201, with its classic water-lily motif bathroom tiles lovingly recreated by the Morinerie Ceramics Studio, and its demure little boudoir and alcove, and the milky light of its alabaster globes.

I now feel duty-bound to disclose a jealously kept secret: the number of my favorite room. A room on the sixth floor, perched on the rooftop prow of this great vessel moored on the rue de Rivoli. Not a large room, but one with a breathtaking

balcony where, in the clouds almost, vertigo-immune lovers can cling to the railings like Leonardo di Caprio and Kate Winslet – even the bathroom has a balcony. Sitting at the writing desk, strategically placed at the very apex of the Regina's hull-like roof, one could almost be inside the head of an insect, looking out through dormer-window eyes on either side: a stereoscopic panorama of Paris, rue de Rivoli and the Tuileries. Room 614.

à deux pas…

- *Sustenance:*

one can of course savor the classical cuisine and very beautiful decor of the hotel's restaurant, Le Pluvinel, but nobody will mind you trying out a few addresses in the immediate vicinity. The excellent and tiny Argenteuil *9 rue d'Argenteuil, 01.42.60.56.22*, for instance, or the imaginative, lively Basque cuisine of Le Dauphin *167 rue Saint-Honoré, 01.42.60.40.11*, one of the best restaurants in the area. You are also in the Japanese area: Kinugawa *9 rue du Mont-Thabor, 01.42.60.65.07* or Isse *56 rue Sainte-Anne, 01.42.96.67.76*.

- *Culture:*

Comédie-Française *1 place Colette* is just there. Mind you, it can be dangerous crossing rue de Rivoli, but once you reach the other side you can easily spend the day in the Louvre and the Musée des Arts décoratifs, *closed Tuesdays*, or relaxing in the Tuileries. Not forgetting that at the Place de la Concorde end of the gardens, you have the Musée de l'Orangerie and the Galerie du Jeu de Paume… The bookshop Junku *18 rue des Pyramides* assures you a trip to mangas world.

- *Couture:*

Regina couldn't be more strategically positioned. The Palais Royal is not far: Didier Ludot *gallerie Valois*, Ibu gallery, Prince Jardinier, Shiseido, the antique dealers… *galerie Montpensier*.

- *The next morning:*

WH Smith's English bookshop or Galignani, along rue de Rivoli near place de la Concorde, has an excellent foreign press section. You can go and read your paper in the Tuileries gardens or at Café Marly next to the Louvre pyramid, *cour Napoléon*, or again at Angelina *226 rue de Rivoli*.

REGINA

2 PLACE DES PYRAMIDES 75001 PARIS

TEL.: +33(1) 42 60 31 10
FAX: +33 (1) 40 15 95 16

E-MAIL RESERVATIONS:
reservation@regina-hotel.com
Website: www.regina-hotel.com

- *Double rooms from 320 to 440 dollars,*
suites from 530 to 765 dollars,
120 rooms and suites
- *Le Pluvinel restaurant*
- *English bar* • *Tea room*
- *8 fully-equipped modular meeting*
or banquet rooms • *Technical equip-*
ment (screens, translators)

Decor
The Regina's lobby, with its lovingly preserved
signs, opalescent green lamps and silver bells,
could almost be a set for a period movie—which
of course it has been.

Atmosphere
It is in the early morning that the Regina exudes its
atmosphere to the fullest; the whole city seems to
resonate in the rich glow of the carpet, the gleam
of a wood panel or the sparkle of a brass wall lamp.

Vantage point
On the mezzanine level snaking the length of the lobby,
set back from the entrance, guests can soak up the
hotel's atmosphere and contemplate the arrivals and
departures of fellow travelers.

Eagle's nest
The great thing about hotels like the Regina is
that none of its rooms are the same. Each one has its
individual role to play, like 614 here, ideally placed at
the corner of the roof overlooking the Tuileries gardens.

WESTMINSTER

— • —

In good hands

First, the location. Think about it: rue de la Paix, the most expensive street on the French Monopoly board; indelibly engraved in the French psyche, as deep-rooted a fixture of the mythic Parisian map as the Champs-Elysées or Place Vendôme. The street that has been there for centuries, one assumes. One imagines Romans parking their chariots here, Huns dismounting for a jug of ale, their horses frothing at the mouth. Nothing of the sort. In 1790 the two-hectare plot was still the vegetable garden of a Capucine convent. Traveling performers set up shop here after the Revolution, and their flea circuses, ventriloquists and phantasmagoria would doubtless have remained by popular demand had not Napoleon decreed that the site was to become "the most beautiful street in Paris." The hotel was built more than a century later, in 1910, but it wasn't until 1930 that it was renamed after the Duke of Westminster, who often stayed there in the mid-nineteenth century, as does the present duke today.

Staff regulations were strict: wine waiters were warned about returning home inebriated and chambermaids had to take chastity vows. It was during these early days that Louis Ferdinand Cartier leased a premises in the building. Since then the jeweler's reputation has grown, but not the thickness of the wall between his shop and the hotel – as if the two old friends didn't want to lose touch with one another.

La Belle Epoque drew to a close, two world wars came and went and the Westminster's clientele changed with the times: the Luftwaffe during the Occupation then a succession of globetrotting travelers, writers and artists. All appreciated the

hotel's very British discretion, so perfectly expressed by the mahogany and marble-columned lobby, with its profusion of majestic flower arrangements, gold leaf and towering ceilings. Everything is stated loud and clear, once and for all, as soon as one enters. The hotel reveals its true self, its rightful sense of proportion elsewhere. The Westminster only really comes into its own in the rooms, whose muffled atmosphere and subtle color harmonies are given a personal touch by engravings, lithographs and drawings. Whereas many of the Paris palaces have sought a dazzling, breathtaking luxury, the Westminster's pursuit of excellence has taken a different course. Its true distinction lies in its focus on the core mechanics and indispensable craft of the great hotels: personalized service. A staff of 125 caters for its 80 rooms and 22 suites. Every room is attended to twice daily by two teams of chambermaids. Every suite has its own butler service. Most of the suites are sponsored by the jewelers in rue de la Paix: Van Cleef & Arpels, Mauboussin, Fred, Chaumet, Cartier, and so on, all of whom offer their own little welcome gift. Each suite also has a marble and bronze clock, inherited from the collection of one the building's previous owners.

The same private, intimate dimension is to be found in the bars and restaurant.
The Céladon's gourmet cuisine (in a previous life the restaurant was a grill room
called the Bulldog) has won the acclaim of the specialist guides, but it is definitely
in the Duke's Bar (until recently the Chenets Bar) that the Westminster gives its very
best. If you have to go through the restaurant to reach the bar (the entrance is in rue
de la Paix not in rue Daunou), you may take a certain malicious pleasure at the
spectacle of the businessmen at table there, sitting in self-imposed detention in front
of their amuse-gueules, those strange little culinary trinkets designed to open up the
appetite (why not get straight to the point and eat?). You, unbeknownst to them, will
be having an equally impeccable meal in the bar, the sole difference being that there
won't be any beating about the bush. You will be served promptly, efficiently and
pleasantly, in the company of those in the know like you.

As you enter the bar with its deep green armchairs you will be struck by the
splendid gothic fireplace. It was moved to the Westminster from the building next
door in 1913. Two of the four figures sculpted on its corbels, Madness (above the bar)
and, in particular, Work (the man with a hammer personifying the stonemason and

builder), epitomize the paradoxes and juxtapositions that are the key to the Westminster's peerless charm. One is constantly passing from one extreme to another. When you go through the doors of the Westminster you leave the city bustle outside, putting the spells of the rue de la Paix's jewelers' windows behind you. You are entering a different, less frenetic environment, a world where everything has been subtly slowed down for you, discreetly taken care of. You hardly notice what good hands you are in.

à deux pas…

- *Food-wise:*

the hotel's Michelin-starred Le Céladon restaurant is major league, but tables in the Duke's Bar are just as sought after because the food there is simple and good and the venue quite chic. But only a few steps away you also have Alain Senderens' Lucas Carton *9 place de la Madeleine, 01.42.65.22.90* and Alain Dutournier's Carré des Feuillants *14 rue de Castiglione, 01.42.86.82.82*. And if it's good food in a prestigious historical setting you're looking for, then try Restaurant du Palais-Royal in the Palais Royal *110 galerie de Valois, 01.40.20.00.27* or the traditional Grand Véfour *17 rue du Beaujolais, 01.42.96.56.27*.

- *Ballet:*

the Palais Garnier is two minutes walk away. The hotel's concierge may be able to help you with last-minute tickets, otherwise you can always try on 01.44.73.13.99.

- *Toys:*

you are only a stone's throw away from Paris's most prestigious toyshop, Le Nain bleu *406 rue Saint-Honoré*.

- *Department stores:*

just the other side of the Opéra, five minutes walk away, there they are, side by side: Galeries Lafayette *40 boulevard Haussmann*, Printemps *n°. 64*, Conran, Habitat, Gap and Zara on boulevard des Capucines.

- *Rocks:*

you are surrounded by the city's top jewelers – Cartier is in the same building as the hotel, and at the end of the street you have Place Vendôme, Paris's jewelry Mecca.

- *Breakfast:*

at the end of rue de la Paix, buy your paper at one of the newsstands on Place de l'Opéra, then breakfast on café and croissants at the Grand Café at the Grand Hôtel.

WESTMINSTER

13 RUE DE LA PAIX 75002 PARIS

TEL.: +33 (1) 42 61 57 46
FAX: +33 (1) 42 60 30 66

E-MAIL RESERVATIONS:
resa.westminster@warwickhotels.com
Website: www.hotelwestminster.com

- *Rooms from 440 dollars,*
suites from 740 to 2650 dollars,
102 rooms, 18 suites
- *Céladon gourmet restaurant*
- *Duke's bar*
- *5 reception rooms*
- *Cigar lounge* • *The Westminster*
- *Fitness Club*

Duke's Bar

Every hotel has its heart. The pulse of the Westminster
is the Duke's Bar, which not only has an excellent
collection of whiskies but also serves quality lunches
supervised by the chef of the hotel's gourmet
restaurant, the Celadon.

Club

The Westminster gives the impression of being run
like a private club, where one is in the company of a
few friends intent on the good life: One appreciates
the excellent restaurant, naturally, but also other
essential fixtures such as this cigar chest.

Working out

The hotel's health club, divinely housed
under the eaves.

Steam

The Westminster is a master at slowing life down,
either by simply giving you breathing space or,
here, enveloping you in the rejuvenating mists
of its hammam.

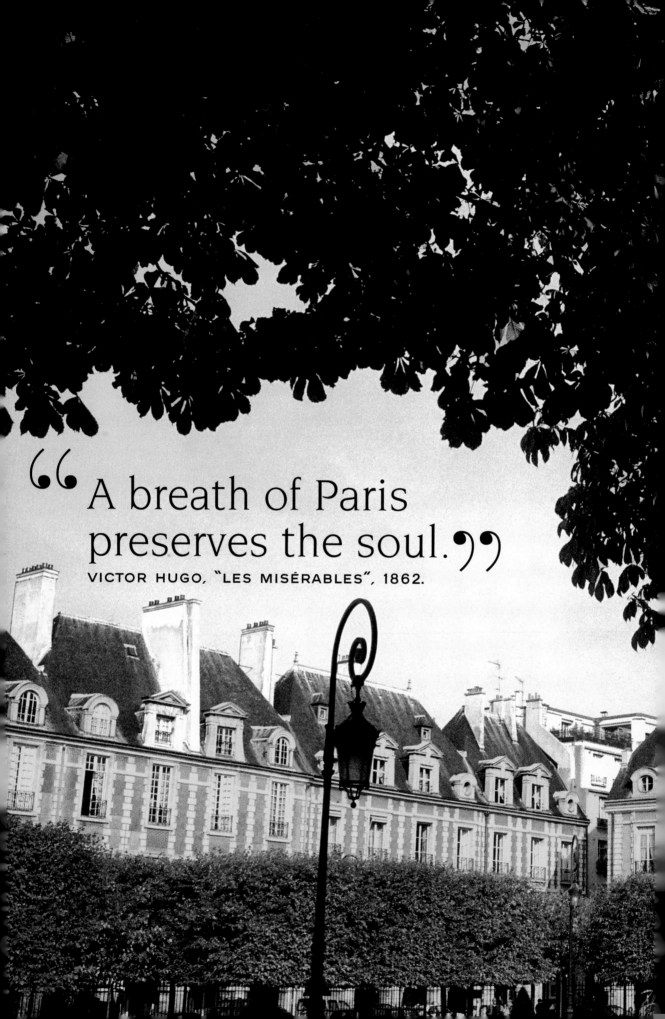

"A breath of Paris
preserves the soul."

VICTOR HUGO, "LES MISÉRABLES", 1862.

PAVILLON DE LA REINE

—◆—

The not-in-a-hotel experience

No view of the Eiffel Tower, hardly any view at all,
yet you are right next to one of Paris's most regal sights,
the Place de Vosges. Is there any need to remind you just
how haunted by historic figures the square is? On a cold
night in November like this, one can easily imagine one
of its most famous inhabitants, Victor Hugo, hurrying
along one of the vaulted arcades in his frock coat,
preoccupied by the next chapter of Les Miserables.
Richelieu and Bossuet were also residents of this royal
housing project built by Henry IV in the early
seventeenth century. Right from the beginning, Place
Royale, as it was then called, was one of Paris's most
sought-after addresses. In 1800 the square was renamed
Place des Vosges, in honor of the Vosges département,
the first to pay its taxes.

The Pavillon de la Reine is set back from the square
itself. Go through the vaulted hallway and then, like
Alice, open the glass door – and suddenly you are in a
quiet little garden, surrounded by bushes, ivy and the
smell of freshly cut grass. If you shut your eyes you could

almost be in the country. The city on the other side of the glass already seems remote. You haven't even set foot inside the lobby, yet somehow you feel you've already been welcomed. You cross the garden and enter the hotel itself. A fire is burning in the large fireplace in the lounge on your right. Later you'll go sit in one of those deep armchairs and watch the flames, or perhaps enjoy a drink at the honesty bar. And just as outside you had the feeling you were already being welcomed, here now is someone coming out from behind the reception desk to welcome you.

The gesture is typical of the hotel. The Pavillon de la Reine does away with lengthy preambles and comes right out and says it: "We like our guests to feel they are in a private home." You've heard the same worn-out refrain a hundred times, nearly always said with too much emphasis and tralalala. Yet somehow you know that here, for once, you're being told the truth. The central concern of the team of women running the hotel is to provide tranquility and privacy. There is no visitors' book, and you needn't bother asking: one of the secrets of the Pavillon's perennial popularity lies in those politely sealed lips. But there are clues, at least to the wide variety of people who stay here. The rooms, for instance, 55 of them and all different.

A mood or theme can be found to match your stay: the exposed beams of 12? the copper canopy bed in 47? the velvety, violet, gray and brown boudoir of the uncompromisingly contemporary 18? And you can shake off imaginary followers in the narrow, winding corridors.

Like all hospitable homes, the Pavillon is always prepared to take in passersby, people who have lost their way. Wanderers already staying elsewhere, overcome by the charm of the Marais, the city's most ancient district, often return that very evening with their luggage. The hotel doesn't have a restaurant. But does it need one? You are here to discover the surrounding area, where two restaurants stand alone.

One is Italian, L'Osteria, on your left on your way up rue de Sévigné (n°. 10 – there is no sign outside). The Venetian chef, Toni Vianello, makes the best risotto in Paris and, in season, razor clams you'll remember for the rest of your life. But closer, under the arcades of the Place des Vosges itself, you have one of the best restaurants in Paris, Bernard Pacaud's L'Ambroisie. The décor, dreamed up by François Joseph Graff, is like a Florentine antechamber. The Pavillon de Reine, L'Osteria and L'Ambroisie have that same sense of intrigue, the same taste for enigma in common. It's as if Paris, afraid of being found out, for just one evening put a finger to its lips and whispered, "Shhhhhhhh..."

à deux pas…

- *Eating around:*

the hotel has no restaurant but just outside, under the square's vaulted arcades, you have one of Paris's most talked about eateries, Bernard Pacaud's Ambroisie *9 place des Vosges, 01.42.78.51.45*. There is also an excellent Italian restaurant, Osteria *10 rue de Sévigné, 01.42.71.37.08*, close by. One of Paris's finest Japanese restaurants, Isami *4 quai d'Orléans, 01.40.46.06.97*, is within easy walking distance. If you prefer a Parisian bistro, then try La Bourgogne, opposite the hotel *19 place des Vosges, 01.42.78.44.64* or La Guirlande de Julie *25 place des Vosges*. Also nearby, the superb Repaire de Cartouche *8 boulevard des Filles-du-Calvaire, 01.47.00.25.86* or, in the same league, Villaret *13 rue Ternaux, 01.43.57.89.76*.

- *The Marais/Bastille connection:*

you can start with the antique shops in the arcades around the square, then move on to the designer boutiques along rue des Franc-Bourgeois, the chic Marais quarter's main shopping artery, but a foray in the opposite direction could be even more rewarding. Some of France's trendiest young designers have set up shop in the streets beyond the Bastille: Isabelle Ballu & Moritz Rogosky, Ladies & Gentlemen, *4, passage Charles-Dallery, on rue de Charonne*, Isabel Marant *16 rue de Charonne*, Shine *30 rue de Charonne*, and the gentle and subtle Anne Willi *13 rue Keller*. The smart address is Azzedine Alaïa *7 rue de Moussy*. Just after, you can buy all kind of teas at Mariage Frères *30 rue Bourg-Tibourg*.

- *Cerebral sustenance:*

the musée Picasso *5 rue de Thorigny*, the Musée Carnavalet, the museum of the city of Paris, *23 rue de Sévigné*, the Pompidou Center *19 rue de Beaubourg*, and Victor Hugo's house *6 place des Vosges, 01.42.72.10.16*.

- *Breakfasting out:*

at the Café des Phares on place de la Bastille. You can also buy croissants at Dalloyau, nearby. Newsstand opposite the café.

PAVILLON DE LA REINE

28 PLACE DES VOSGES 75003 PARIS

TEL.: +33 (1) 40 29 19 19
FAX: +33 (1) 40 29 19 20

E-MAIL RESERVATION:
contact@pavillon-de-la-reine.com
Website: www.pavillon-de-la-reine.com

- *Rooms from 350 to 400 dollars, suites from 440 to 740 dollars, 55 rooms and suites furnished with Louis XIII style period furniture in harmony with the architectural style of Place des Vosges*
- *Private garage*
- *24-hour room service*
- *Dogs accepted*

Details

When space is at a premium, every detail plays a crucial role in creating rooms and bathrooms of irreproachable comfort.

Decor

The Pavillon de la Reine's strength lies undoubtedly in its decoration, essentially old-style French but complemented by charming contemporary touches.

Open arms

As soon as you enter, the Pavillon de la Reine states the theme with its spacious welcoming lounges and "open bar."

Shank's mare

Cars frequently get left in the hotel garage as the majestic Place des Vosges is just outside and the shopping streets of Paris's delightful Marais quarter are near at hand.

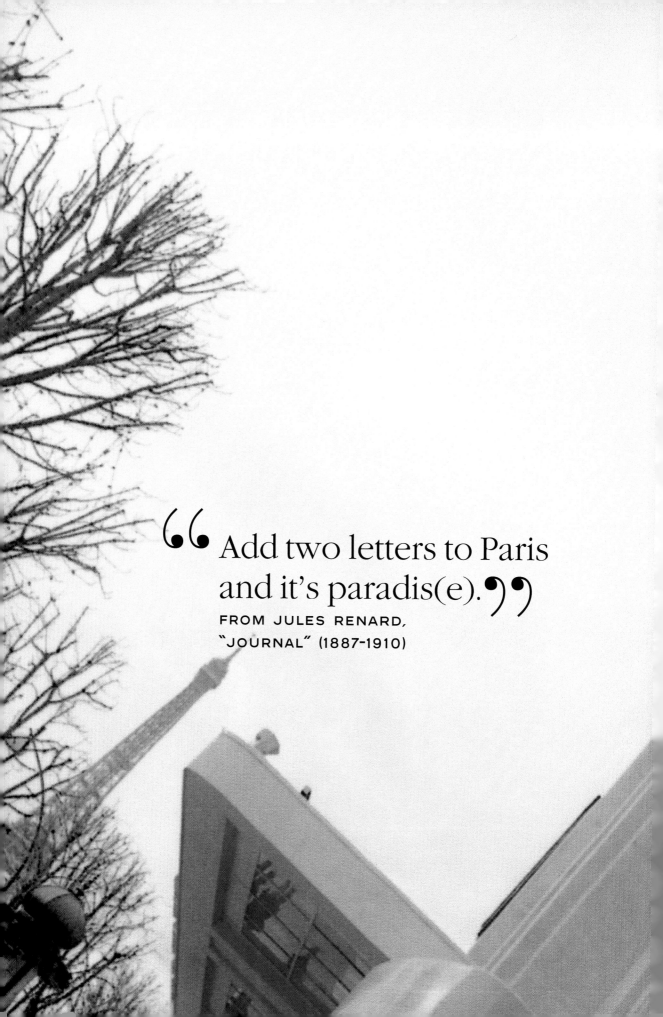

"Add two letters to Paris
and it's paradis(e)."

FROM JULES RENARD,
"JOURNAL" (1887-1910)

PERSHING HALL

Between method and madness

It doesn't take a quantum leap of the imagination. Stand outside Pershing Hall, just off the Avenue George V, and picture the building not so long ago, when it still housed the offices of Paris Match magazine and the French headquarters of the American Legion. In the bar, journalists and paparazzi used to persecute the pinball machines while doughboys reminisced over a beer until media and military packed up and went their separate ways. For years the building stood vacant, waiting, the shutters of the Second Empire facade closed to the outside world. One era had come to an end, another was about to begin. Enter Andrée Putman, the acclaimed interior designer (Morgans in New York, the Ritz Carlton Wolfsburg). When she first visited 49 rue Pierre Charon she was speechless. She could hardly control her excitement. Nothing is more impressive than an empty building.

When the initial, first-impression emotion had blown over, she kept her cool. "I wanted a country feel, a certain provincial freshness; above all, nothing heavy, merely simplification. It took guts to install a vertical garden in the extremely narrow, dark courtyard, to transform it into the hotel's lungs. Now when I return to this hotel I rediscover my original intention to create a secretive luxury, which I did with the very elaborate winged mirrors, the simplest lamps in the world, beds higher than normal to give them more presence, taut window curtains and the washable linen bedside rugs running under the beds."

The hotel unfolds like a tango, in an alternation of poses (beautiful spaces and copper, amber and gray harmonies) and subtle movement (the large bead curtains). The tempo takes a little getting used to but once you get in step you get carried away.

The hotel allows you breathing space, keeps its distance. It doesn't rush or oppress you. Sometimes one needs to be left alone, to have one's silences, one's own tempo respected. There are times when one likes a hotel to forget about you, when one is content to be casually given the keys to one's room (54 for its interior balcony or 24 or 27), and left to muse in peace in a grayish-beige plaid and Mongol cashmere meridienne. As Patrice Lecuiller, the manager, so rightly points out, "We have no right to interfere with our guests' dreams. It's up to us to make them feel at ease."

On the Paris ladder of designer hotels, the top rung will always be the uncomfortable one. But then that's the price of fame in this city – if anything new or different is to be elevated to cult status, then it has to be systematically disemboweled in the process. The ritual is performed almost with a vengeance, as though fueled by some underlying rivalry or jealousy. The Parisian's knee-jerk reaction to something fashionable is like a child's with a piggy bank: break it to see what's inside. All of which whips up media hysteria. A myth is whisked into existence, a volatile cocktail of bitterness, acidic remarks, honey-sweet smiles and daggers in the back.

Pershing Hall's arrival on the scene was no exception. Dancing on razor blades, surfing on a wave of glossy magazine hype, the hotel's reputation rocketed skyward. But a media feeding frenzy is never a free lunch. Infatuation is by definition fickle and ephemeral. Promises to phone each other were made the morning after but... the swallows of fashion were already migrating elsewhere. Chastened, wiser for it all, the hotel was at last left to its own devices. Things settled down, a new, revised Pershing style and a regular clientele began to take shape. Such is the Parisian way of things.

Ascertaining whether any of the mustachioed virility of the original American Legion Pershing Hall persists could take a full weekend. The only salient expression of that madness sought by Andrée Putman is Patrick Blanc's 115-foot-high vertical garden. Jungle is a more appropriate word, because hundreds of different tropical

plants from the Philippines, the Amazon and the Himalayas have been embedded in the felt-covered wall. But don't go expecting Rambo to emerge from the foliage with a machete between his teeth, or that the birds that have made the undergrowth their home were designed by Jacques Garcia, with stripes and fezzes on their heads. No, they are simply humble Parisian sparrows.

à deux pas…

- *Eating around:*

you can opt for the hotel restaurant's pleasant and gently contemporary cuisine but don't forget that you are in one of Paris's culinary hotspots. You are within walking distance of Pierre Gagnaire at the Hôtel Balzac *6 rue Balzac, 01.44.35.18.25*, Alain Ducasse's Relais Plaza and Philippe Legendre's at the George V. But there are also less obvious options such as Spoon, *Alain Ducasse again…, 12 rue de Marignan, 01.40.76.34.44*, Tateru Yoshino's classical French cuisine at the Stella Maris *4 rue Arsène-Houssaye, 01.42.89.16.22*. If you're looking for somewhere more intimate, try Baretto *9 rue Balzac, 01.42.99.80.00*. Parisian bistro lovers should make straight for Le Pichet *68 rue Pierre Charron, 01.43.59.50.34*. But there are others, such as Senso *see La Tremoille, page 145*.

- *Brain food:*

the appetites of the mind can be sated at the Palais Galliera museum, *fashion and painting, 10 avenue Pierre-Ier-de-Serbie*, the Musée d'art Moderne, *11 avenue du Président-Wilson*, the Palais Chaillot *17 place du Trocadéro* and the Musée des arts asiatiques-Guimet *6 place d'Iéna*.

- *Café, croissant, papers:*

to keep your trendy café hand in, you can wend your way down to Avenue Montaigne, newspapers under arm (newsstands on the Champs-Elysées), to L'Avenue *41 avenue Montaigne, 01.40.70.14.91*, a recent Costes brothers creation and one of the chicest hangouts in town.

- *Besieged by boutiques:*

Cartier right next to the hotel, avenue Montaigne: *Prada, Dior, Celine…*, avenue George V: *Vuitton, Agnès Comar, etc.* and the Champs-Élysées only minutes away…

PERSHING HALL

49 RUE PIERRE CHARRON 75008 PARIS

TEL.: +33 (1) 58 36 58 00
TAX: +33 (1) 58 36 58 01

E-MAIL RESERVATIONS:
info@pershinghall.com
Website: www.pershinghall.com

- *Rooms from 400 to 525 dollars,*
  suites from 760 to 1050 dollars,
  26 rooms
- *Fitness center and health spa*
  opening in 2003

Hanging garden

One of the hotel's main attractions is its five-story vertical garden, designed by Patrick Blanc, with its hundreds of tropical plants and the birds who come to sing specially for the guests in rooms 44 and 54.

Food

The hotel's initially extremely inventive and ambitious cuisine has since been tempered to cater to the district's fickle appetites who, it would seem, haven't mourned the change.

Pearls

Andrée Putman, the designer in charge of the hotel's renovation, envisioned "a country feel, a certain provincial freshness." Her large pearl screens bring the lobby to sparkling life whilst softening the solemnity of the architecture.

Well-being

The immaculate clarity of Andrée Putman's bathrooms, with their glass mosaic and Viennese friezes, are a perfect expression of a certain imperious Pershing sense of well-being.

PLAZA ATHÉNÉE

---◆---

Tyranny
of excellence

The Plaza is definitely the most barrel-chested of the Parisian palaces, the one with the most blow. And also the one with the most insolent motto for the new millennium: "Once upon a time there was the hotel of tomorrow." Where did it get all that furious energy, all that muscle? The key to the lung capacity may lie in avenue Montaigne's original name. Before it was renamed after the philosopher Michel de Montaigne in 1850, it was called Avenue of Sighs. But even if the Plaza, since its inauguration in 1911, has never run out of breath, it has hardly ever had a moment to take one. The hotel quickly became one of the world's high-society Meccas. And wherever people in high places congregate, so do spies: Mata Hari stayed here regularly. In which room? – 120, giving onto the courtyard with its geraniums and the snobbiest sparrows in Paris. She was arrested at the Elysée Palace in 1917, but in the 1964 movie *Mata-Hari* starring Jeanne Moreau the scene was shot at... the Meurice.

Lift a spoonful of letters out of the alphabet soup and the Plaza can hang names on them all: Yuri Gagarin, John D. Rockefeller, Jean Cocteau, Charles Lindbergh, Josephine Baker, Stavros Niarchos, the Kennedys... The complete list would run like a trailer preview for The Twentieth Century: The Movie. Herbert von Karajan dined unfailingly at the Relais Plaza restaurant after concerts, always at the same table, nº. 20, in the corner on the left near the stairs. And always ate the same meal:

vegetable soup, sole meunière and a carafe of Bordeaux. And every time he arrived the whole restaurant gave him a standing ovation. The Relais's admirable and terrifyingly classy and discreet headwaiter, Werner Köchler, could talk about such things for hours but of course prefers to do even better: just look you in the eyes and say nothing. The man has seen it all. For it should be said that daily the Relais puts on one of the most delectable and inimitably Parisian floor shows of them all – the airs of lazy prosperity, the fur-lined solitude, men caught in Dow Jones, FTSE 100 or CAC 40 dramas who, once the news has sunk in, realize they may not now be able to die with their pockets full, that this may be the last time they ever dine at the Plaza, in this magical decor, like an ocean liner run aground.

The Plaza is a volcano forever erupting, an endless lava flow of passion in pursuit of excellence. Then François Delahaye arrives, changes the carpets and redoes the bathrooms. One of France's greatest chefs, Alain Ducasse, arrived at the Relais amidst a media fanfare. The result was predictable. The restaurant on avenue Montaigne went galloping out ahead of the pack, snatching all the prizes: Best Hotel Bar in the World, three Michelin stars, Best Club Sandwich... The Plaza exudes

excellence from its every pore. You can't escape it, it's everywhere: in the geraniums in the courtyard (which are used to make a cocktail), in the magical hands of the masseur in the health spa, in the bubble gum-flavored ice cream milkshake with vodka and wild strawberries in the bar.

Reeling, intoxicated by all this excellence, you go upstairs expecting to be bathed in milk and honey, to find yourself on Mount Olympus or sitting on a sofa from the Vatican. You've been promised a rose garden, the moon... instead you're brought down to earth by six floors of rooms (188 in number) in the purest French classical style. Louis XV, Louis XVI and Regency furniture, period fabrics, moldings and fireplaces (with built-in plasma screens and video) – and, miraculously, it isn't boring. Everywhere, warm, comforting touches manage to save it all from feeling like a museum: shimmering quilted taffetas, bouffant folds, tinted soft furnishings, deep pile carpets, period lamps, gold-lined silk lampshades on the chests of drawers, bedside lampshades lined with yellow doupion silk. On the seventh and eighth floors, Art Deco returns with sketches by the great couturiers and in the duplex suites such as 150 with its private terrace looking out over the Eiffel Tower and its private health

spa. Showbiz people adore the suite, apparently. Names? "Mick Jagger," you are reluctantly told after an exasperated sigh.

It would be so easy to shut oneself up in the Plaza forever, to succumb to its spell, but that would be to forsake the magic that the Plaza is merely a part of, the city beckoning outside.

à deux pas…

- *Gastronomy:*

need one look further than the hotel itself? After the consummately classical cuisine at Alain Ducasse's three-Michelin-star Plaza Athénée restaurant, one can try the Relais Plaza, also one of Paris's most sublimely "Parisian" venues, where not only the food but the clientele is worth the sitting. If you are in the mood for something more informal around lunchtime, try the club sandwiches and other snacks at the Galérie. But it would be a shame to shun avenue Montaigne, which boasts La Maison Blanche *15 avenue Montaigne, 01.47.23.55.99*, ideally situated above the Théâtre des Champs-Élysées, the view is superb, as is the restaurant's elaborate cuisine, and L'Avenue *41 avenue Montaigne, 01.40.70.14.91*, where you will again encounter the Costes brothers' much-imitated, *because imitable* lively "snack" dishes. You can also venture into the surrounding streets, which are some of Paris's most impressive restaurant-wise *see George V, Lancaster, Pershing Hall, etc.*.

- *Brain fodder:*

the Drouot Montaigne auction house, Christie's, the art galeries on Faubourg-Saint-Honoré and on avenue Matignon, the Théâtre des Champs-Élysées *ask the concierge for the concert program* and the Palais de la Découverte *avenue Franklin-Roosevelt, 01.56.43.20.20*.

- *The Golden Triangle:*

the lineup along avenue Montaigne is vertiginous *Calvin Klein, Apostrophe, Prada, Dior, Celine, etc.*, then comes avenue George V with *Vuitton, Agnès Comar* and the Champs-Élysées… not forgetting, of course, the parfums of Caron *34 avenue Montaigne*.

- *Terrace breakfast:*

those who overcome the temptation to breakfast in-Plaza have merely to cross the avenue and have breakfast at Bar des Théâtres *6 avenue Montaigne* for a change. Newstand on place de l'Alma.

PLAZA ATHÉNÉE

25 AVENUE MONTAIGNE 75008 PARIS

TEL.: +33 (1) 53 67 66 65
FAX: +33 (1) 53 67 66 66

E-MAIL RESERVATIONS:
reservation@plaza-athenee-paris.com
Website: www.plaza-athenee-paris.com

- *Double rooms from 525 to 790 dollars, suites from 830 to 6400 dollars, 145 rooms, 43 suites and a duplex*
- *Private fitness club and sauna*
- *The Plaza Athénée (Alain Ducasse) restaurant*

Stars
Three-Michelin-star Plaza restaurant led by Alain Ducasse continues to ride high in the French restaurant firmament but one can opt for the simplified rigor of his Relais Plaza, still the most Parisian of the great Paris restaurants.

Bars
The Plaza bar, a tour de force of biting modernity and one of Paris's most sublimely elegant, was recently voted one of the top hotel bars in the world.

Rooms
In mid-suite, a staircase beckons you heavenwards whilst preserving the spirit of the classic Parisian bourgeois interior.

Feeling better
Nowhere can one escape the Plaza's tyranny of excellence, least of all in the hotel's health spa, where the masseur is reputed to have magic hands.

BRISTOL

---◆---

The silent hotel

In 1923, when the foundation stones of the Bristol were laid, everyone thought the project was bound to fail. Whatever did its 31-year-old owner, Hippolyte Jammet, think he was doing, erecting a palatial luxury hotel out in the middle of nowhere? Cows were still driven up rue Verte alongside the site. And, to compound his folly, he had demolished a magnificent Renaissance mansion, the Hôtel de Castellane, to build his palace. But the righteous indignation was short-lived. He was by no means the first property developer to commit such a sacrilege, nor would he be the last. And, as we will see, there was method in Monsieur Jammet's madness.

The superb new edifice went up in record time. The newborn was christened le Bristol and the name hastily hung up outside – and then promptly blew down one windy day. The descent of the sign was, of course, an omen. The name Bristol, it was claimed, was not Monsieur Jammet's to use. The battle to establish the name's rightful ownership went to court, but this didn't prevent the young man, undeterred by such a minor legal snag, from supervising the finishing of the Bristol's monogrammed crockery. And the courts found in his favor. He could do as he had always intended to do, name his hotel after the Comte de Bristol, who, beside being a widely traveled and extremely demanding eccentric (like so many of the Bristol's future clients), was also the bishop of Cloyne. Hippolyte Jammet was intent on making the Bristol into Paris's equivalent of the fabulous Adlon in Berlin, and he used every high-tech means at his disposal. He even installed an "air-cleaning machine," a precursor to the air conditioner. Unfortunately, the ammonia-guzzling beast made almost as much noise as a steam train, and technicians regularly passed out from the fumes.

Our headstrong young-man-in-a-hurry was a visionary hotelier. He invented the mirophare, a revolutionary pivoting mirror magically lit from within (but was in too much of a hurry to patent it). He was an innovator in every field to make his hotel like none other: in each room, a fresh mahogany toilet seat, sealed in its plastic wrapper, greeted every new client until 1978. But perhaps the Bristol's true singularity lies in its sparseness, in the absence of visual clutter. One is given space and light rather than tapestries or frescoes. The Bristol prefers to keep a respectful distance, to discreetly maintain its Carrara marble decorum. It is known as the hôtel du silence, above all for its sense of discretion, its exemplary unintrusiveness.

However, all manner of wishes can be and are catered to. One client asked for the walls of his room to be covered with thousands of daisies for his wife's birthday – her name was Daisy. Another American couple, anxious that their children should continue their schooling, requested that a room be transformed into a schoolroom. And when blackboard, chalk and desks had been duly installed, they announced that their children's teacher and classmates were being flown over from the United States. There are, of course, quieter clients. Naomi Campbell, before she bought an apartment in Paris, regularly stayed at the

Bristol, always in 964, renowned for its extraordinary 200-square-meter terrace. Where of course she sunbathed to the delight of the 100 or so rooms opposite – one of which, 729, has another view almost as spectacular. Lie there at night and gaze out at the Eiffel Tower, center frame, directly in line with the bed, sticking up like a luminous capital "I." Ample consolation for not being able to stay in the legendary Panoramic Suite, non?

Unlike many hotel restaurants, who bend over backward to ensure year-round constancy, the Bristol likes to ring in the changes of season. Each November, when the hunting season begins, you can count on not only game but the reopening of one of the most beautiful dining rooms in Paris, the "Winter Restaurant." If you want to dine in its summer counterpart, which the ever-so-respectful Gallimard guide comically describes as a "garden shelter," you'll have to wait until April. The description doesn't do justice to this sublime oval dining room, once a small theater, with its honey-colored Hungary oak woodwork and

ceiling frescoes painted in 1940 by Gustave-Louis Jaulmes (who decorated the Salle Pleyel concert hall). And so things would have continued year in year out if the Bristol hadn't parachuted Éric Fréchon into this sumptuous decor. Trained at the Crillon (during the Constant period) and flushed with the success of his bistrot-restaurant in the 19th arrondissement, Fréchon concocted an exciting blend of both – palace cuisine (mile-long dish names and multi-digit checks to match) and ingenious mouth-watering little dishes. It's still in its early days, but already praises are being heaped upon the new Frechon Bristol.

A straight-faced hotel, definitely, even a slightly straight-jacketed one, but, as you'll discover if you go up to the sixth floor, also one that knows how to let itself go. In the quasi-surrealist swimming pool styled like a yacht lying at anchor on the roof, Sacre Coeur on one side, Eiffel Tower on the other, you can float in turquoise-blue waters, gazing out over frescoes of Cap d'Antibes and, beyond the pine trees, the Eden Roc.

à deux pas…

- *Eating in and out:*

first things first: the Bristol's excellent restaurant which, under Éric Fréchon's tutelage, has forged a cuisine midway between traditional French provincial and rigorous classicism. But the district is hardly lacking in culinary heavy-weights, such as L'Angle du Faubourg *195 rue du Faubourg-Saint-Honoré, 01.40.74.20.20* and the ambitious annex of Taillevent *15 rue Lamennais, 01.44.95.15.01*. Another of my favorites is Chez Catherine *3 rue Berryer, 01.40.76.01.40*, for its elaborate bistro cuisine and fine wine list. For a lighter, more discreet business lunch, Chiberta *3 rue Arsène-Houssaye, 01.53.53.42.00*.

- *The street of streets:*

nothing could be easier. Rue du Faubourg Saint Honoré awaits you with open arms. Step outside, turn left and let the street sweep you away like a magic carpet…and if you manage to reach the Comédie-Française without reaching for your credit card, then you are one of the iron-willed few. But the ordeal has only just begun: you now have to return to the hotel via the chocolates of Jean-Paul Hévin *231 rue Saint-Honoré*, Colette, Goyard, Gucci, Hermès, Lanvin, Yves Saint Laurent, Versace…up to Christian Lacroix, just in front of your hotel.

- *Between boutiques:*

visit the numerous art galleries in the area *avenue Matignon, faubourg Saint Honoré…*

- *Next day:*

you can enjoy a nice breakfast at Dalloyau *10 rue du Faubourg-Saint-Honoré*.

BRISTOL

112 RUE DU FAUBOURG SAINT-HONORÉ
75008 PARIS

TEL.: +33 (1) 53 43 43 25
FAX: +33 (1) 53 43 43 26

E-MAIL RESERVATIONS:
resa@hotel-bristol.com
Website: www.hotel-bristol.com

- *Double rooms from 500 to 750 dollars,*
  suites from 800 dollars,
  127 rooms, 48 suites
  - *Restaurant* • *Working space*
    - *Reception rooms* • *Bar*
      - *Swimming-pool*
    - *Health club* • *Beauty salon*

Tea bar

Where else could France's august tea drinkers' club
meet to sip their favorite beverage from delicate
porcelain cups? But rest assured, other drinks and
light lunches are also served at the bar, hence its
popularity with businessmen.

"Salle d'hiver"

Éric Fréchon's reputed cuisine is more than a match
for the Bristol's superb oval winter dining room with
its Hungary oak paneling and ceiling frescoes
painted by Gustave-Louis Jaulmes.

Suites

The Bristol's star attractions are its suites and
apartments: 964 has a vast 200-square-meter terrace,
but the others are just as spacious.

Secret garden

Who would expect to find such a large garden only
blocks away from France's presidential palace
and the Champs-Elysées? As soon as weather
permits, the restaurant quits its winter
quarters to spend the summer here.

GEORGE V

A new season,
a new reign

In 1997, when the George V was stripped of its contents and its insides ripped out, a century was reduced to rubble and dust. Only afterward, standing in the numb silence of the vast cavity inside, did one realize just how much had disappeared; only then did the enormity of the loss finally sink in. History had been taken away by the truckload; legend, reduced to shattered masonry and mangled debris, had been carted away for landfill; settees, four-poster beds, even the salt cellars had gone up for auction. The haunting presence of Greta Garbo, Vivien Leigh, Gene Kelly, Brian Jones and John Lennon had vanished into thin air. All that remained was a gaping hole.

Inaugurated in May 1928, the George V was the brainchild of its owner, the American architect Joël Hillman. With an ideal location in the heart of Paris, the - nine-story, white stone art deco palace had been designed as a "private residence," whose comfort, dignity and elegance would appeal to a high-society clientele – primarily, Americans in Europe for the Grand Tour. And the hotel more than lived up to its regal name. General Eisenhower even chose it as his headquarters in 1944 during the Liberation of Paris. And now, as befits such an august, historic institution, it has risen again –zap! bright as a button– from its own dust. Once again a trilingual commissionaire is there to usher you through the doors of the George V –excuse me, the Four Seasons George V– recently voted Top International City Hotel.

Yes, the George V is back with a vengeance, with all the gnawing ambition of the "first in the class," ever eager to tyrannize us with its excellence. An excellence that assaults you as soon as you enter the lobby: the Sienna yellow, gray and beige marble, the Regency mahogany presentation table surrounded by capacious Empire armchairs with gold velvet upholstery, the crystal and bronze chandelier... not to mention the white marble statues of the four seasons. And, of course, the floral decorations. Among Paris's finest, they are the work of American-born Jeff Leatham. A former top model, he went on to become the florist at the Los Angles Four Seasons before Didier Le Calvez, director and orchestrator of the Paris resurrection, brought him over for the reopening of the George V. Jeff stayed on in the City of Lights and now has 15,000 blooms brought from Holland each week for his ten arrangements in the lobbies and 150 bouquets for the reception desks and tables throughout the hotel.

And when sights have been set for the stars, the restaurant could hardly be less than heavenly. The rare and exquisite combination of chef Philippe Legendre's cuisine and Eric Beaumard's wine list have lost no time in propelling the George V's reputation for haute gastronomie back into high orbit. But there were inevitable casualties. In its quest to reinvent its excellence, the George V did away with its art deco heritage. Everything, apart from the Salon Chantilly and the guardrails on the windows, has been replaced by a designer hybrid, a genetically engineered "marriage between the French classical style and the quality standards of a luxury hotel of international reputation."

Of course, the George V's brand new excellence has its matching clientele, all members of the same tribe of impatient, demanding world nomads. Elusive figures who arouse a murmur of recognition as they flit from limo to elevator. Or who accidentally drop their pink portable mini-stereo in the lobby. The victim of this scandalous misfortune, the nonagenarian English novelist Barbara Cartland, demanded that her miniaturized ghetto blaster immediately be replaced. Paris –the whole of Europe– was scoured for the petite pink machine, to no avail. Finally, a special envoy was sent to the factory in the United States. When he returned with the adorable little thing, the pink lady hardly even acknowledged the feat. And never set foot in the George V again.

The occupant of the next room, another very rich, very old lady, demanded that her newspaper be brought to her hand-sewn. "May I ask why, madame?" "So that the pages

don't fall out while I read it, of course." "I quite agree, madame, nothing could be more disagreeable." The devil, as always, is in the details, and this is precisely why the George V is so worthy of our boundless esteem. Admittedly, there is that rather irritating insistence on being perfect, but there is fortunately that (almost) human touch, a certain tenderness that renders this bearable. In the midst of such perfection, one doesn't expect to suddenly slip into a world of tender glances and warm smiles over a perfectly chosen wine, to marvel at the soft leather on the tables, or the exquisite arabesques of a flower arrangement. For those who know how to wait for it, who are on the lookout for it, the George V knows how to come down off its cloud and give the best of itself down here in this world – albeit a world of pink marble, silver salvers and oven-gilt brioche. And like us all, the George V knows full well that in a world where everything is possible, everything inevitably becomes a tiny bit boring. And this is why, caught in this awkward dilemma, the George V has taken it into its head and heart to go just that bit further, to venture where no hotel has ever gone before, to take you into the unexplored yet oh-so-very-real world of the Four Seasons George V.

à deux pas…

- *Eating in and out:*

be aware that the hotel you have chosen is obsessed with the quality of its restaurants. When the George V reopened, Philippe Legendre, the excellent chef at Taillevent, and Éric Beaumard, one France's finest wine waiters, were enlisted to deliver a high-flying classical cuisine. One can also have a pleasant meal in a neighboring room, seated on comfortable settees. Avenue George V has more to offer in this genre, in the form of Flora Mikula's newly opened restaurant *01.40.70.10.49*. And of course at the top of the avenue, on the corner of the Champs-Elysées, there is the legendary Fouquet's *01.47.23.50.00*, ever-faithful to its banal cuisine and self-obsessed clientele. Seafood lovers will reserve at the consistent but slightly overrated Marius et Janette *4 avenue George-V, 01.47.23.41.88*. And remember that you are close to Pierre Gagnaire *6 rue Balzac, 01.58.36.12.50* one of France's major talents.

- *Shopping:*

stop by Hédiard, downstairs in the hotel, if you fancy sweet flavours. See also the neighboring Plaza, Pershing Hall, Tremoille, etc.

- *A new day:*

as all hotel aficionados well know, nothing beats sneaking out to breakfast at another. Where? The Plaza Athenée, of course *see page 102*

- *Brain food:*

the Drouot-Montaigne auction house, Christie's, the Théâtre des Champs-Élysées, *ask the concierge for the concert program*, the musée d'Art moderne *11 avenue du Président-Wilson*, the musée Guimet *6 place d'Iéna*, and soon the musée Baccarat on place des États-Unis.

GEORGE V

31 AVENUE GEORGE V 75008 PARIS

TEL.: +33 (1) 49 52 70 00
FAX: +33 (1) 49 52 70 20

E-MAIL RESERVATIONS:
www.fourseasons.com

- *Rooms from 700 to 950 dollars,
suites from 1300 to 9500 dollars,
245 rooms including 61 suites*
- *Restaurant* • *Bar and tea room*
• *Business facilities
with a capacity of up to 600*
• *Fitness center*
• *Health spa and swimming pool*

Gastronomy

Philippe Legendre, the hotel's talented head chef,
is also in charge of the George V's room service,
the bar and, of course, the hotel's flagship restaurant, le
Cinq, directed by the excellent Eric Beaumard.

Wine cellar

Deep in the bowels of the hotel, carved out of the Paris
bedrock itself, the hotel's impressive wine cellar.

Flowers

Ex-model Jeff Leatham was brought over from
California to oversee the flower arrangements when
the George V was reopened. Enchanted by his stay
in the city, he stayed for good.

Care

When the George V puts its mind to something
(cuisine, flowers, rooms), one has the impression
it wants to be more than merely the best. The
hotel's obsession with excellence is continually
seeking new heights, as the hotel pool illustrates.

CRILLON

—◆—

Living a little

"The book is sleeping, don't wake it up."
Serge Gainsbourg (the Crillon visitor's book)

If it's history you're looking for, the kind you read about in history books, then you've come to the right place. The Crillon has seen it all —revolution, decapitation, consecration, liberation— then seen it again. If it happened in Paris then it probably happened here, if not inside these very walls then outside those windows. For more than two centuries history has been unpacking its suitcases here, demanding quail and rose sorbet in the middle of the night, sleeping, waking and having continental breakfast.

Upstairs, in the first-floor salons or the presidential suites behind the neoclassical facade, looking out over Place de la Concorde, you'll inevitably have that feeling you've forgotten something. Your scepter, your tiara, your gem-encrusted shoes perhaps? But there's no need to worry, the abundant staff are here to reassure you, to remind you that there is only one real king at the Crillon: the guest.

The Crillon's history is daunting, like a too-rich layer cake, like a meal with too many courses (the digestion of which you, the guest, is spared). For a starter, the signing of the Treaty of American Independence in 1778. The Comte de Crillon bought the magnificent edifice soon afterward, but then had to leave the capital to save his skin. Heads were rolling in the square outside. The Revolution came and went; the count returned, and to cut a long story short, the river of history continued to flow until, in 1907, the building was acquired by the Société des Grands Magasins

et des Hôtels du Louvre. The company intended to turn it into one of the finest hotels in Europe. Paris had at last decided to get its act together. Soon the French capital's prestige hotels were vying for the favors of the world's rich and nouveau riche. The Grand Hotel was renovated in 1904, the Ritz and Meurice had begun their irresistible ascension and the palaces on the Champs-Elysées were hard on their heels. And here they are a century later, still locked in the same battle for supremacy.

You only have to look out from the Crillon's grand siècle salons to understand why Paris is considered by many to be the most beautiful city in the world. The view is almost too sublime to be true, like a movie set. Exterior, Paris, sunset: the Place de la Concorde surrounded by a symphony of sublime silhouettes, the Eiffel Tower, gilded domes, statues and classical porticos, with the Tuileries gardens stretching away to the left and the Champs-Elysées to the right. From the top-floor rooms (the Bernstein suite) the panorama is even more breathtaking. The suites were recently refurbished and now have free access to the terraces. I remember the time when one was reluctantly entrusted with a key to a sliding security grille with the solemn

warning: "Don't open the grilles too often, don't lose the key, do be careful."

The sheer overwhelming power of the Crillon experience can leave no one indifferent. A stay there bathes Paris in an entirely new light. But beware, such exaltation can drive guests to distraction. Like some distant ancestor of a rock star, the Russian poet Sergei Alexandrovitch Essenine, in a fit of rage, "trashed" his suite, tearing down curtains and throwing furniture about. It took several policemen to overpower the colossus. His wife, the legendary dancer and turn-of-the-century icon Isadora Duncan was outraged by the press coverage. The incident had (mistakenly) been headlined as "yet another marital tiff." Today's stars are more than accustomed to the tabloids' excesses. "If this goes on," Isadora Duncan protested, "your journalists will soon be opening coffin lids to describe the dead person's expression."

In the restaurant, the superb Ambassadors' Room, rarely has a napkin been cast down in anger. For the simple reason that the cuisine is one of the most traditional of all the Parisian palaces. Which is the table of tables? Table 14, at the back of the magnificent room, by the windows. At lunchtime the sun shines in on a superb gilded Baccarat crystal bowl. This is the table of Jean Taittinger, the chief executive of the hotel group, and also of Roxane Debuisson, the grande dame of French gastronomy. For the last twenty years she has eaten in Paris's luxury hotel restaurants almost daily. The wine is always discussed prior to her arrival in one of her five Rolls Royces. Not that this is really necessary: whether she lunches alone or with company, a bottle of Dom Ruinard champagne is always there waiting, nestling in its bed of ice and rose petals in the Baccarat crystal bowl. Once, for April Fool's Day, a mischievous headwaiter (since promoted) discreetly placed a goldfish in the bowl. Roxane Debuisson is undoubtedly the only person in Paris to know the surname and first name of all the waiters and kitchen staff at the Crillon (pastry cooks included).

à deux pas…

- *Food:*

the Crillon's restaurant, Les Ambassadeurs, is renowned for its classicism, and the hotel also has the more everyday Obélisque, but no one will frown on you for eating around in the vicinity. True, there is always the moving decadence of Maxim's *3 rue Royale, 01.42.65.27.94,* but you need only go along to La Madeleine to encounter Alain Senderens' more high-spirited and just as prestigious cuisine at the Lucas Carton *9 place de la Madeleine, 01.42.65.22.90.* If you're looking for a bit more conviviality and life, though, opt for brasserie Flottes *2 rue Cambon, 01.42.60.80.89,* La Ferme des Mathurins *17 rue Vignon, 01.42.66.46.39* or the more trendy Hôtel Costes *see page 22.*

- *Brain food:*

you merely have to cross rue de Rivoli to savor the riches of the Louvre, the Musée des Arts décoratifs *closed Tuesdays* or, closer, on Place de la Concorde, the Musée de l'Orangerie *Monet's Water-lilies* and Jeu de Paume exhibition gallery.

- *Breakfast:*

you can either cross the Seine for a terrace breakfast on Place de l'Assemblée Nationale or remain on the Right Bank and go along rue Royale to the patisserie and salon de thé at *n°. 16,* Ladurée, which has a newsstand directly opposite.

- *Ear, nose and throat:*

there is a pharmacy in rue Boissy d'Anglas.

- *Shopping:*

immunity to the myriad temptations of rue du Faubourg Saint-Honoré is rare, but if you do succumb, it may well be at the shoemaker Rodolphe Ménudier, *14 rue de Castiglione,* whose stiletto heels leave no one unmoved.

CRILLON

10 PLACE DE LA CONCORDE 75008 PARIS

TEL.: +33 (1) 44 71 15 00
FAX: +33 (1) 44 71 15 04

E-MAIL RESERVATIONS:
reservations@crillon.com
Website: www.crillon.com

- *Double rooms from 580 dollars, suites from 960 to 7250 dollars (Bernstein suite), 90 rooms, 57 suites (including 3 presidential ones)*
- *Les Ambassadeurs restaurant • L'Obélisque restaurant • Bar*
- *8 reception rooms • Guerlain beauty salon • Fitness club*

Marble

Marble everywhere, an endless sea of it stretching from the lobby into the dining rooms (in particular the Ambassadors' Room), giving this palace its dreamlike quality, its disconcerting smoothness.

Breathtaking

One of the Crillon's greatest assets is of course its breathtaking views of the Place de la Concorde. Paris seen like this, in all its timeless majesty, can seem unreal, almost like a stage set.

Emotion

The penthouse suites are the jewels in the Crillon crown. The Bernstein, one of the most sought after, has its own grand piano and private terrace looking out over the Place de la Concorde.

Bathrooms

The Crillon is currently entirely renovating all its rooms. A batch of 23 brand new rooms with discreetly modern bathrooms came on line in January 2003.

LANCASTER

Time regained

"I want to be alone."
Marlene Dietrich, suite 45

The true luxury of the Lancaster lies in its authenticity and confidentiality. One would hardly be surprised to see a "Do Not Disturb" sign on the door of this stately townhouse built in 1889, so close to the throng of the Champs-Elysées yet so discreet, withdrawn almost. The lobby, with its iroko wood furnishings, is a model of contemporary dignity, yet you still have that nagging feeling you've stepped into a time warp. You can almost see the horse-drawn carriages arriving, hear the clatter of hooves as they drove through the entry hall and deposited their passengers in the courtyard beyond (now the garden), before turning and leaving.

Originally the Paris mansion of Santiago Drake del Castillo, the building remained in the family until it was bought in 1925 by the Swiss hotelier Emile Wolff. He immediately set about converting it into a hotel, wisely enlisting his talented housekeeper, the daughter of a renowned antique dealer, to help him with the furnishings. She was given carte blanche to fill the Lancaster with a remarkable collection of antique furniture, eighteenth-century wall clocks, paintings, Baccarat crystal chandeliers and valuable fabrics, and the duo lost no time in making the Lancaster one of Paris's most sumptuous hotels. So much so that at the beginning of World War II, as the Wehrmacht was advancing across western France toward the capital, the German High Command already had designs on it. But Emile Wolff had other ideas. He raised the Swiss flag of neutrality on the first-floor balcony, and the Lancaster was left in peace throughout the Occupation. The hotel might well have freewheeled through the rest of the century, resting on its laurels like so many of its Parisian counterparts, had its path

not crossed that of another peerless hotelier. In 1995 Grace Leo-Andrieu (responsible for the revamping of the Bel-Ami and the Montalembert in Paris, the Clarence in Dublin and the Cotton House Resort on Mustique island) took over the management. Inexorably, the Lancaster's charm had been wearing off. Its savior, the daughter of a Hong Kong hotelier, was called in just in the nick of time. An adept of Feng Shui, she immediately identified where the hotel's chi (its vital energy) lay and located where it was trapped or stagnating. The reception desk had been hidden away at the back of the ground floor. She brought it nearer, but not too close to the entrance. The revolving door, symbol of a bygone age (in which clients regularly got stuck with their luggage), was done away with. But Grace Leo-Andrieu was only too aware that one can't go tampering with places like the Lancaster at will. If new energy was to be breathed into the magnificent old lady it had to be done with velvet gloves, with all the deftness of a silversmith. A large mirror was installed in the lounge to circulate light – something, incidentally, which no Feng Shui adept would ever do in a bedroom (for fear of interfering with sleep). And in the garden a little brook was sent babbling over gray-beige and white pebbles.

But fear not, the Lancaster's spirit hasn't transmigrated. Nor has its furniture evaporated in the auction rooms. They still reign, priceless heirlooms with all their imperial subtlety. For

those who have time to appreciate it, the hotel is a model of refinement, a delightful hopscotch skipping from one century to another, from classic modern design to fascinating curios to eighteenth-century furniture. Everywhere one looks, the eye is intoxicated with exquisite details, with sheer style. In suite 75, for instance (Jeremy Irons's favorite), with its cinema-scope balcony views of Paris, the bathroom is a hymn in white and ivory marble, stone, sponges and leather. Other spirits still haunt the Lancaster. Quietly, on tiptoes almost, you approach the door of suite 45, the door on which Marlene Dietrich once left the message, "I want to be alone," and also the door underneath which a note was once slipped, saying, "Madame, I have taken your wish into account. Here, served with ice, is the bartender you requested." Dietrich's daughter lived along the corridor, in room 48. In her autobiography she wrote about her mother's many lovers, the men who were shown to this door on numerous occasions, or only once. Nowadays, the management is reluctant to discuss the licentious legacy left by one of its most legendary guests. It is deemed more interesting to mention how her daughter was always awed by the fact that she never encountered a chambermaid. It was as if the rooms were cleaned by magic. Or it is thought preferable to dwell on how much Marlene Dietrich loved Paris, how her interior decoration tastes were similar to Marie Antoinette's. She loved

mauve, violet and pale pink and had a soft spot for trinkets and knickknacks, particularly
Chinese objects. To have brought a hotel like the Lancaster into the next century with its soul
still intact is no mean feat. Grace Leo-Andrieu believes that a hotel should never be left to its
own devices. Like a top athlete, excellence lives to be put under pressure: "The Lancaster is
at its best when it is full, when clients are demanding, when we are kept on our toes. When
one is too relaxed, things come undone, one loses one's touch. The charm wears off." The

restaurant, which had been for guests only, was opened to the outside world. Au revoir the old private dining room, bonjour to the twenty-first-century public coming in from the street. And the cuisine, too, has risen to this self-imposed challenge. The food is modern and light, with a cutting-edge culinary touch. The Lancaster threw down the gauntlet, challenged itself to a duel. It knew it had nothing to fear, the force was with it, the force of those spurred on by their own legend, who enjoy galloping out in front with the competition snapping at their heels.

à deux pas…

- *Eating in and out:*
the hotel restaurant was recently placed under the guruship of Michel Troisgros *Roanne, maison Troisgros* and opened to the public. But if you're looking for a little more intimacy or somewhere quiet to do business, try Chiberta *3 rue Arsène-Houssaye, 01.53.53.42.00*, where the cuisine is lively and incisive. In the same vein, there is also Laurent *41 avenue Gabriel, 01.42.25.00.39*, whose cooking and service is impeccable. Lasserre *17 avenue Franklin-Roosevelt, 01.43.59.02.13* belongs to the same distinguished, aristocratic family of restaurants, as does Ledoyen *1 avenue Dutuit, 01.53.05.10.01*. Otherwise, in the classic crowded Parisian brasserie genre, Le Bœuf sur le Toit *34 rue du Colisée, 01.53.93.65.55* is about as good as it gets.

- *Brain food:*
the art galleries in and around avenue Matignon; the exhibitions at the Grand Palais *3 avenue du Général-Eisenhower*, the Palais de la Découverte museum *avenue Franklin-Roosevelt* and the Petit Palais museum *avenue Winston-Churchill*.

- *Ear, nose and throat:*
there are pharmacies all along the Champs-Élysées.

- *Hair care:*
Opalis, specialist for personal cares, will offer you a nice relaxation *63 rue de Pouthieu, 01.45.62.51.56*.

- *The next day:*
ideally, one should buy one's croissants at Ladurée *75 avenue des Champs-Élysées* or savor them over coffee at Fouquet's *n°. 99*, which has a newsstand opposite.

LANCASTER

3 RUE BOULAINVILLIERS 75016 PARIS

TEL.: +33 (1) 44 14 91 90
FAX: +33 (1) 44 14 91 99

E-MAIL RESERVATIONS:
hotel.square@wanadoo.fr
Website: www.hotelsquare

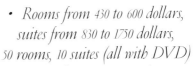

- *Rooms from 430 to 600 dollars,*
- *suites from 830 to 1750 dollars,*
- *50 rooms, 10 suites (all with DVD)*
- *24-hour room service*
- *Movie library*
- *Reception rooms for private dinners*
- *Meetings and conferences*
- *Health club • Sauna • Parking*

Salons

One of the Lancaster's delights is the miraculous peace of its vast lounges, only a stone's throw from the Champs-Elysées. The armchairs and settees are as soft as the silence. The lounge once rang with the clatter of hooves as carriages entered the hotel courtyard.

Greenery

The hotel's most poetic touch is its garden, with its parasol of fern fronds, grayish beige pebbles and white Burgundy flagstones.

Master touch

The Lancaster saves its trump card for its rooms, where Grace Leo-Andrieu, who masterminded the hotel's facelift, has managed to preserve all the hotel's original stately grandeur whilst introducing subtle touches of modernity.

Bathroom test

Another good way of gauging a hotel is by its bathrooms. The Lancaster's are serene, well ventilated affairs, bathed in the soft light of white glass mosaic.

LA TRÉMOILLE

Brand new body, same old soul

Deep in the heart of the Golden Triangle between avenue Montaigne, avenue George V and the Champs-Elysées, lies a hotel perched discreetly on the corner of rue de la Tremoille and rue Boccador. A curiously self-effacing hotel, eyes closed to the outside world, almost as if it wanted to be forgotten. Or could the Tremoille still be suffering from post-renovation trauma? Nothing could be more understandable: the hotel recently had its insides ripped out and its furniture auctioned at Drouot. Yes, appearances can be deceptive: behind that facade is an entirely renovated, brand new Tremoille. Once upon a time there were 107 rooms, now there are 93.

It should be said that the Tremoille had lost the plot somewhere along the way. But then this has been the lot of many a great hotel that has passed from hand to hand, from whim to whim. It started life as a private residence in 1883,

became a hotel, then was bought by Charles Forte in 1968 (along with the Plaza Athénée and the George V) and now belongs to The Scotsman Group.

Augustin Benedetti, the Tremoille's director since 1966, is still wiping his glasses, taking stock of things, rather like his recently renovated hotel. One needs time to recover one's emotional bearings. But throughout, his hand has remained firmly on the helm. The same unwavering Tremoille creed, the same sense of purpose persists: "The Tremoille exists above all for its regular clients. That's why, despite the exceptionally long renovation period, our team is unchanged. We are here to further the Tremoille spirit, to honor the legacy of fidelity our regular clients have bestowed on us. I still remember Michel Audiard" –the legendary French screenwriter– "who stayed here Monday to Friday, always in the same room, no. 510. He would receive actors and directors in the dining room. It was like being in a film. Lino Ventura would arrive, to be joined by Jean Gabin or Louis de Funes. De Funes was another regular guest: room 409–410. And few people knew he indulged in his favorite pastime there, playing the piano. We succeeded in getting a baby grand up the narrow staircase for him. But then the hotel has always been a favorite of musicians: Isaac Stern, Rostropovitch, Yehudi Menuhin... We are not far from the Théâtre des Champs-Elysées and we can provide them with the peace and serenity so vital for their work."

There are, of course, regulars and The Regulars, those serial Tremoille habitués who have often spent extended periods of time here: Lee Marvin, Tony Curtis, Gene Wilder, Richard Gere, Orson Welles, Philippe Noiret. "But Sting has also stayed here," Augustin Benedetti adds. As have the Red Hot Chili Peppers: a bemused neighbor called one night to warn Benedetti that a group of bearded figures were fooling around on the roof. Another regular roof user, four-legged this time, went by the name of Norton. Whenever the American author, screenwriter and Tremoille regular Peter Gethers came to work in Paris –with Roman Polanski on *Frantic* (starring Harrison Ford), for example– he always came with his cat. He wrote a book about Norton's adventures, *The Cat Who Went to Paris*. Norton held court in the great restaurants (L'Ambroisie, Robuchon, and so on) and was a revered regular in the nightclubs (Les Bain Douches). Peter Gethers considers

the Tremoille exemplary of that very French tolerance for animals. He loved the hotel, felt like "a duck in water" there: "It's gorgeous," he wrote, "It is small, it is elegant, it is very Parisian, and they love my cat."

There was a time when customers at the Tremoille's Louis d'Or restaurant, hankering after a change of menu or décor, could finish their meal at the George V or the Plaza on the same check because the three hotels belonged to the same owner.

But many a bottle of Chambertin has flowed under the bridge since. Hardly shedding a tear, the Tremoille has turned over a brand new leaf. Gone without trace is that outmoded feel guests once found so touching; modernity, cutting-edge technology is now here in force. Behind that discreet, exquisite facade, a charm offensive was launched to seduce a whole new generation. The rooms are now bathed in tawny, ochre and brown tones, their acoustic insulation is impeccable, their air is replaced every few seconds, and a modem socket is always within easy reach. Mission accomplished: the revamped Tremoille has attracted a new, often business clientele.

And, curiously, even the name, La Tremoille, is losing its old-world singularity. The word belongs to that rare breed of quaint old relics that are not pronounced as they are spelled. As Broglie is pronounced Breuille, Tremoille is pronounced Tremouille. But the usage is, it seems, now on its way out. Tremoille, a "knight above reproach," was one of the great men of the French Renaissance. He was born at Thouars in 1460, during the reign of Louis XI. The commander of an army of 12,000 men, he fought the Dukes of Britanny and Orange. He fought at Venice, Dijon and Marignan and pacified Normandy before being shot through the heart at the battle of Pavie.

Observant regulars will have noticed that the hotel's shield, which once depicted the noble lord peacefully mounted on his charger, now shows him on an elegantly rearing steed, an equestrian pose more in keeping with the ambitions of today's Tremoille. And nowhere is the hotel's new spirit more spectacularly in evidence than in the restaurant, Senso, conceived and designed by Terence Conran, with a contemporary global fusion cuisine that is nevertheless anchored in Parisian tradition.

A new page has been turned, but the book remains the same. The views from the fifth and sixth floors are still just as breathtaking (rooms 608 and 615 have views of the Eiffel Tower), and the spectacular bow windows of the 01 rooms remain. The hotel also has another feature, unique in Paris: each room has an outer and inner door, enclosing a room service "hatch" in which meals, linen or polished shoes can be left without disturbing the client. The Tremoille has leapt resolutely into the twenty-first century, body and soul.

à deux pas…

- *Eating out:*
the recently renovated hotel now hosts Sir Terence Conran's second Paris
restaurant venture, the trendy and good-value Senso. But there is no
shortage of pricey designer-concept restaurants in the area: the excellent
chinese restaurant Diep *55 rue Pierre-Charron, 01.45.63.52.76*; la Maison Blanche
15 avenue Montaigne, 01.47.23.55.99 has a superb view; Nobu *15 rue Marbeuf,
01.56.89.53.53*; the inventive Shozan *11 rue de la Tremoille, 01.47.23.37.32*; le Stresa
7 rue Chambiges, 01.47.23.51.62, the smartest italian restaurant in Paris; and
Alain Ducasse's Spoon *14 rue de Marignan, 01.40.76.34.44*.

- *Soul food:*
the Drouot-Montaigne auction house, Christie's, the art galeries on avenue
Matignon, the Théâtre des Champs-Élysées, *ask the concierge for the concert
program*, the Musée d'art moderne *11 avenue du Président-Wilson*.

- *The Golden Triangle:*
all for men: the shoes of Berlutti *2, rue Marbeuf*, the specialist for nice
cashmere Hobbs *45 rue Pierre-Charron*; and for women: Charles Bosquet
13 rue Marbeuf; salon of Marc Delacre *17 avenue George V…*
Without forgetting the best chocolates in Paris at Fouquet *22 rue François Ier*,
and the forthcoming opening of the perfume shop By Terry in rue de la
Trémoille.

- *Morning after:*
go to Place de l'Alma and pick your café terrace and newsstand. Delicious
hot chocolates in la Maison du Chocolat *56 rue Pierre-Charron*.

LA TRÉMOILLE

14 RUE DE LA TRÉMOILLE 75008 PARIS

TEL.: +33 (1) 56 52 14 00
FAX: +33 (1) 40 70 01 08

E-MAIL RESERVATIONS:
reservation@hotel-tremoille.com
Website: www.hotel-tremoille.com

- *Double rooms
from 430 to 590 dollars,
suites from 610 to 1000 dollars,
88 rooms and 5 suites.*
- *Restaurant*
- *Bar*
- *Health club*

Restaurant
The hotel's new restaurant on the ground floor, Senso, designed and managed by Sir Terence Conran, owes its success to its artful fusion of world cuisine anchored in traditional French gastronomy.

Bathrooms
Along with everything else in the building (whose interior was recently entirely rebuilt from the ground up), the bathrooms were completely redesigned.

Facade lift
The hotel's facade, with its superb balconies and columns of bow windows was also renovated.

Hatch
The hotel has an original room service system consisting of a "hatch" between each room's outside door and inner door, in which staff can leave meals, linen or shoes without disturbing guests.

"Reading time is always stolen time: that is probably why the metro turns out to be the biggest library in the world."
DANIEL PENNAC, "COMME UN ROMAN", 1992

CONCORDE SAINT-LAZARE

The return of a grande dame

Be warned: when you go into the Concorde Saint-Lazare, make sure you're not carrying a breakable object or engaged in an urgent conversation. When you enter you will be struck dumb, your eyes will open wide and your will jaw drop. Your expression will surprise no one. The receptionists, who have you in their sightline as you enter, won't even bat an eyelid. They're used to seeing the same first-time visitor routine replayed daily – the brief intake of breath, the slowing to a standstill, that stupefied, gawking gaze first upward then around you, at the majestic cathedral-like space inside.

But this wasn't always so. More than a century ago, expectant travelers flocking here from all over the world arrived above you, entering directly from the Saint-Lazare train station by an overhead gangway. The Grand Hôtel Terminus (as the Concorde Saint-Lazare was then called) would have been virtually the sole subject of conversation on

the train journey that brought them directly from the transatlantic ports of Le Havre and Cherbourg. As the hotel's mainly foreign clientele sped to Paris from the coast, they knew that a temple of luxury and refinement awaited them. It was said that a stay in the Grand Hôtel Terminus, or even merely visiting it, was enough to justify the long voyage to France.

Back in the 1880s, foresighted entrepreneurs realized that there was a dire lack of modern luxury hotels for visitors to the 1889 Paris World's Fair. They lost no time. A monumental hotel, designed by Juste Lisch (and inspired by Gustave Eiffel), was erected in a record fifteen months and inaugurated on May 7, 1889. The magnificent edifice was fully equipped with the latest technology (electricity, telephone) and furnished throughout by Les Grand Magasins du Louvre. The idea was that the client had everything instantly at his or her fingertips: telephone, cloakroom, hairdresser, restaurants, delicatessens and luxury-goods shops.

Hotel staff were waiting to greet you on the platform as the train slowed to a halt. You were then ushered across the overhead gangway (still there but today no longer in use) that led directly into the sumptuous hotel lobby. "When I arrive at Saint-Lazare station," a Grand Hôtel Terminus brochure assures us, "a porter takes my travel ticket and leads me straight into the hotel. I'm already in bed as my fellow passengers wait fretfully on the pavement below, haggling with cab drivers and porters. And then, before my departure, my ticket is brought to me and my luggage checked in without me so much as leaving my room. Still in slippers, pajamas and dressing gown, I cross the gangway directly to my sleeping car: no waiting in the cold, no fret, no fatigue. I've saved time, money and trouble."

The original mirrors, framed by marble arcades and columns, still line the hall; the same crystal and bronze chandeliers still sparkle in the glass ceiling. But that once familiar feature of fin-de-siècle and belle-époque train stations, the murals glorifying the railway's illustrious destinations, have sadly been painted over. The superb cherubs, on the other hand, were spared. Don't miss the one with his back sulkily turned on us, a little jewel. The artist, Carlo Lameire, disgusted after a dispute over his pay, begrudgingly completed the commission but only thinly veiled his feelings in his work. Paris is full of similar artistic expressions of pique, the Arc de

Tiomphe itself being no exception. The sculptor Jean-Baptiste Carpeaux, persecuted for his homosexuality, left us his triumphant last word in stone: indelibly carved into this monument to the virtues of the French Republic is a young soldier sporting a magnificent erection.

The tradition has always been that hotels with such meteoric beginnings spend the following century digesting their dazzling past. The Concorde Saint-Lazare was no exception. Like some diva with a hangover, still in her nightgown, she spent the next hundred years contemplating her past glories – while the rest of the world moved on. Ocean liners had become too slow, fashion's whims and cycles accelerated. By the 1980s our great lady was a ghost of her former self. In her now tattered nightgown, she spent her days mumbling half-forgotten arias to herself. The big-city bustle only yards from her door (the Gare Saint-Lazare is one of the busiest stations in the world, in the same league as Tokyo's Central Station) would have continued to pass her by if not for one of the station's minor destinations: a small village on the Seine. Today Monet's (no longer so) peaceful country retreat at Giverny remains one of France's top tourist destinations. Americans and Japanese daily tramp the length and breadth of the

painter's modest residence. The kitchen, with its magnificent blue and yellow crockery, and the garden, with its famous lily ponds, can be as crowded as the Gare Saint-Lazare during rush hour. Monet left for Giverny from these same platforms, and now his devoted admirers have brought color back to our diva's cheeks. The old Chesterfields in the lobby were replaced by spectacular ochre, plum and pine-green meridiennes designed by Herro. The ailing grande dame was given a long-awaited sniff of smelling salts. She awoke with a contemporary feel, a new sensuality. Lisch would heave a long sigh of relief at the audacious changes made. Color —ochres, browns, reds— returned to those corridors as long as station platforms. But, as is often the case with those upon whom the world has turned its back for too long (and who have shut themselves off from the world in return), that original magic has returned only tentatively, on tiptoes. Timidly, it haunts the Golden Black Bar; sometimes it is there to be tasted in the restaurant's resolutely traditional cuisine. Hopefully, if one waits in the hall long enough, the diva's soul may again take up permanent residence in this bustling quarter of fleeting comings and goings.

à deux pas…

- *Dining out:*

the hotel restaurant is pleasant and the food impeccable, but if you're looking for somewhere more Parisian then you don't have far to roam. In the immediate vicinity, you have Chez Jean *8 rue Saint-Lazare, 01.48.78.62.73*, run by an ex-Taillevent chef, the adorable Velly *52 rue Lamartine, 01.48.78.60.05* and Dominique Versini's Casa Olympe *48 rue Saint-Georges, 01.42.85.26.01*. In the same street, there is also an excellent Breton restaurant, Ty Coz *n°. 35, 01.48.78.42.95*, and even a sixties theme bistrot called Georgette at n°. 29, *01.42.80.39.13*.

- *Shopping around:*

five minutes walk away, behind the Palais Garnier opera house, there they are side by side, Paris's two major department stores: Galeries Lafayette with its excellent food hall *40 boulevard Haussmann*, and Printemps *n°. 64*. You can also rummage the racks for Jean-Paul Galutier or Gianfranco Ferre at the Parisian temple of designer seconds, L'Annexe des Créateurs *19 rue Godot-de-Mauroy*.

- *Ear, nose and throat:*

there is a comprehensive pharmacy opposite the hotel.

- *Café, croissants:*

roam around the district and pick a terrace to match your humor or, if you're in the mood, go watch Parisian commuters milling through Saint-Lazare station, one of the busiest in the world – the croissants aren't quite as good, though…

CONCORDE SAINT-LAZARE

108 RUE SAINT-LAZARE 75008 PARIS

TEL.: +33 (1) 40 08 44 44
FAX: +33 (1) 42 93 01 20

E-MAIL RESERVATIONS:
stlazare@concordestlazare-paris.com
Website: www.concordestlazare-paris.com

- *Rooms from 420 to 520 dollars,*
  suites from 725 to 965 dollars,
  226 rooms, 40 suites
  (one presidential suite)
- *Café Terminus restaurant*
- *24-hour room service*
- *Bar*
- *Conference room*

Wee hours
One often expects a hotel to draw out the night, to make it linger in the sparkle of a glass or the gleam of a lacquered bar top, as here in the Golden Black Bar, where night takes its time, gives you time to shed the cares the city before retiring to you room.

Restaurant
At the end of an exhausting journey or a tough day, not in the mood for anything too elaborate, you may well opt for the hotel restaurant's reassuring down-to-earth French cuisine.

Yesteryear
Once upon a time travelers arrived directly from Saint-Lazare station and the Atlantic ports across this footbridge, which is today unused.

High time
The hotel has at long last breathed new life into its previously insipid rooms. A touch of modernity and warm colors have been injected into their original period decor.

RAPHAËL

The hotel on the hill

When you enter the Raphaël, the hotel conceals its game, or at least hangs back. It's as if you were walking into a carefully laid ambush. The reception desk is set away to the left, at a more than respectful distance, as though shying away from you, pretending not to be there. The same thing strikes you upstairs. When you walk the corridors, as you tread the secretive purple Aubusson carpets of this "family manor house" built by Léonard Tauber in 1925, you wonder, Where is everyone? Yet you know there's no need to worry. The occupants of the 90 rooms (including 37 suites) merely have to lift a finger and a major-domo immediately appears at their command. Back downstairs again, in the English-style bar with its honey-colored woodwork, one has the same strange feeling of having the hotel to oneself: everyone seems to know each other yet no one acknowledges one another's presence. You lift a finger, ask whether your guest has arrived yet. "I will inquire, sir."

The secret of the unique Raphaël atmosphere is, of course, inherited, a simple matter of breeding. Flashback to the early twentieth century, to when Léonard Tauber first muscled his way into the elite ranks of Paris's luxury-hotel pioneers (Ritz, Wolf, Jammet, Schwenter *et al.*). In quick succession he created the Régence (300 rooms) in 1900 and then raised the stakes with the Majestic in avenue Kleber, one of the most dazzling palaces of the period (which was subsequently sold to the French state before it became an international conference center). But Tauber also had in mind an even more refined, vaster hotel for his transatlantic guests and their families and retinues: the Raphaël (he was a passionate art lover). His architect, Rousselot, was commissioned to realize his most extravagant dreams. Each sumptuous suite had hand-painted paneling, priceless silk wall hangings and murals depicting the Paris parks or eighteenth-century pastoral scenes.

But the apotheosis of this decorative furor is to be found on the fifth floor, in a quasi-hysteria of bookcases, alcoves and recesses, such as the little chess room with its hidden niche. All of which almost pales into insignificance next to the Raphaël's supreme decorative element, one many Paris palaces are deprived of: Paris itself. When you open the windows, the full beauty of the city explodes in your face – the sea of blue roofs, the pomp of its Haussmann architecture and the city's eternal sights, Montmartre, the Arc de Triomphe and the Eiffel Tower. The Raphaël is a hilltop palace; its hanging gardens and balconies are at the same altitude as the top of the Arc de Triomphe. For your information, room 601 looks out over the Arc, 608 over the Eiffel Tower, 621 over Montmartre, and the Raphaël Suite over the whole lot, courtesy of a 360-degree view. Little need, therefore, to explain why the Raphaël has always had a long list of regular guests. And little need to explain that if celebrities return here again and again it's for the privacy not the paparazzi (the service entrance on rue Lapérouse is regularly staked out).

One such regular was Mishima, who plumbed the depths of solitude here before he committed suicide in Japan. The numbers of his favorite rooms all ended in 7. But therein lies the magic and mystery of all hotels. They harbor so many more secrets than our familiar haunts, and guard them even more jealously. Each of a room's successive guests has the illusion he is the first, that his loves, woes, trials and tribulations are being written on a clean slate. One client, with monogrammed shirts and special soaps, vacates the room for the next, who is allergic to silk and has brought his own pillowcases...

It is no wonder why Federico Fellini, Walt Disney, Roberto Rossellini, Romy Schneider, David Bowie, Ava Gardner, the Kennedys, Burt Lancaster, Vladimir Horowitz, Jean-Luc Godard, Paul McCartney, Gina Lollobrigida and Harold Lloyd all stayed here. Marlon Brando needed the protection of the Raphaël while he was shooting *Last Tango in Paris*. And how many hotels would have waited night after night for Serge Gainsbourg to finish playing the piano in the bar, before eventually

giving him the keys so he could let himself out on his own? Or —back in the sixties now— what other suite could have been the love nest of Katherine Hepburn and Spencer Tracy than 609, like a movie set with its balcony overlooking the Arc de Triomphe and the Paris Opéra? Everything is still there just as it was, ready for new romances as fiery as theirs. Alone in your room, lying on the bed, you don't even have to close your eyes to imagine it all: the awful admissions, poisonous lies and passionate kisses, the hopes kindled or dashed, the hearts that stopped... The German author Ernst Jünger, who stayed at the Raphaël during World War II, recounts how dissident German generals plotted here. They were called the Raphaëlites.

This morning, the hotel's resident cabinet maker has a little problem in room 402 to attend to. The doors of the enormous wardrobe are sticking a tiny bit. The doors are a symptom of one of his constant headaches. Everyone has his or her own idea of the ideal room temperature. The night before a young lawyer from Boston lowered the temperature to 15° C. But the night before that an Italian couple from Ravenna had raised it to 22° C... and, of course, the wood of the period furniture creaks and groans accordingly. Improvements at the Raphaël have always been made little by little, as

discreetly as possible. Like an organism, the Raphael's cells are constantly being invisibly replaced (all of the Raphaël has been entirely renovated since 1985). A long-term policy made possible by the hotel's long-term ownership by the same family (also owner of the Regina and the Majestic). The Raphaël's unique atmosphere has remained perfectly preserved because of this continuity. The hotel's team of decorators and art and bronze restorers are constantly maintaining the original atmosphere, making sure that each stay here is a moment of eternity.

à deux pas...

- *Sustenance:*

the hotel restaurant, in the classical, serious style, is well worth a visit.
Nothing show-off or eye-catching here, simply perfect bourgeois poise. But
if you are intent on something more spectacular, then it has to be either the
breathtaking and visionary Pierre Gagnaire *6 rue Balzac, 01.58.36.12.50 - you'll
have to reserve some time in advance, though,* or the more classical and reserved
Alain Ducasse at the Relais Plaza *see page 96.* Taillevent *15 rue Lamennais,
01.44.95.15.01* is unconditionally admired by many for its professionalism,
while Les Élysées at Hôtel Vernet *25 rue Vernet, 01.44.31.98.98* is going from
strength to strength since the recent arrival of Eric Briffard. But don't forget
Le Cinq at the George V *see page 114.* And for a change of register, try the
genteel bistro Tournesol *2 avenue Lamballe, 01.45.25.95.94*; le Prunier
16 avenue Victor-Hugo, 01.44.17.35.85 for its historic decoration, or l'Étoile
12 rue de Presbourg, 01.45.00.78.70 for its unique outlook.

- *The Golden Triangle:*

on avenue Victor-Hugo: Apostrophe, Hobbs, Céline, Yves Saint Laurent...
Lemaire et la Boutique 22 for their excellent cigars!

- *Brain fodder:*

the Drouot-Montaigne auction house, the Théâtre des Champs-Élysées
concert hall *ask the concierge for the program*, the Musée d'art moderne
11 avenue du président Wilson.

- *The next day:*

just seat down at the terrasse of the delicious bakery Carette *4, place du
Trocadéro*; numerous newsstands on that same square or just in front
of the hotel, waiting for the reopening of the Publicis Étoile Drugstore
on l'avenue des Champs-Élysées.

RAPHAËL

17 AVENUE KLÉBER 75016 PARIS

TEL.: +33 (1) 53 64 32 00
FAX: +33 (1) 53 64 32 01

E-MAIL RESERVATIONS:
reservation@raphael-hotel.com
Website: www.raphael-hotel.com

- *Double rooms from 445 to 530 dollars, suites from 700 to 3500 dollars, 53 rooms, 37 suites*
- *Roof garden at the same level as the Arc de triomphe* • *The Salle à Manger gourmet restaurant*
- *Health spa*
- *Traditional sauna*

Reception

The Raphaël's reception desk, set slightly back from the entrance, symbolizes the hotel's discreet but ultra-professional efficiency.

Bar

The Raphaël's bar is one of those deceptively intimate places where Parisians come to recognize each other without acknowledging one another's presence.

Rooms

An invisible in-house army of craftsmen – picture and bronze restorers, decorators, etc. – is permanently at work restoring, renewing and maintaining the Raphaël's fabric and atmosphere.

Hilltop views

The Raphaël's terraces are extraordinary because they are so unexpected. Not only do they host one of Paris's most fashionable restaurants during the summer months but also one of the most spectacular views of the city.

SAINT-JAMES

Far from the madding crowd

"Thank you. See you often."
Jean-Louis Trintignant

You feel strangely buoyant, lightheaded, like one of the hot-air balloons that used to rise from here in the 1890s. You almost feel like pinching yourself. You have to remind yourself where you really are, to tap yourself on the shoulder and say, "No, you are not in the garden of a château on the banks of the Loire." Yet neither are you really in Paris. You are at the Saint-James.

The site was Paris's first aerodrome before Madame Thiers, the widow of former French president Adolphe Thiers, built a magnificent mansion here to house a foundation in memory of her husband. The idea was that France's finest young minds and most brilliant scholars should be freed of material worries to further their studies in the sciences, philosophy and history here. France's former first lady stipulated, "And above all, politics should have nothing to do with the creation of this school, which should be imbued with a grandeur in keeping with the man to whom it is consecrated." From 1893 to 1980 some 450 laureates, including Georges Huismans, the founder of the Cannes Film Festival, the philosopher Michel Foucault, the historian Alfred Grosser and the jurist Maurice Duverger, spent five years living in this academic Garden of Eden. And today, in the paradise of the Saint-James, that illustrious past, that selfsame rigor in pursuit of excellence lives on.

When one enters the Saint-James for the first time one is struck by the sheer verticality of the main hall with its soaring staircase. You are in one of the most

beautiful interiors in Paris. In the rooms, initially remodeled by Andrée Putman, the same airy loftiness is present in the surprisingly narrow and high inner doors – no doubt intended to echo the languid, very British rigor of the vast two-story library, now the hotel bar. Instead of leafing through one of 12,000 Morocco-bound volumes surrounding you –most of them devoted to law and algebra– try consulting the list of more than seventy whiskies. In the "blue hour" of early evening, the huge leather Chesterfields fill up with one of Paris's most select clienteles, drawn here by the confidentiality and security of a club (the restaurant is for members and guests only) but also by the sheer beauty of the tall airy room itself and that vivacious, inspired feeling it bestows on its occupants.

The 48 rooms take up where downstairs left off, echoing the same inspiration throughout. The new life Andrée Putman breathed into them in the 1980s (even the bathrooms, with their period taps and fittings, crenellated with Viennese friezes, exude the same serene energy) has been complemented by Philippe Hurel's furniture and exciting new touches. Here again, one is enchanted by the constant play of space and light – the hopscotch of dormer windows in 509, for instance. The fifth floor, with its

interior terraces separated by curtains, is a delight to the eye and senses. When you arrive on this sun-drenched platform, you could almost imagine you were in the Hospices de Beaune. The effect is almost playful, yet utterly efficient.

The movie director Luc Besson, inspired by the succession of staircases, shifting atmospheres and climates, transformed the Saint-James into the Russian Embassy in *La femme Nikita*. He wrote the script for the movie here, too – although the Saint-James would never tell you this. A long line of famous writers have written here before him, one is informed, but the Saint-James obstinately declines to divulge their identities, just as a mistress doesn't name former lovers she continues to hold in her heart.

à deux pas…

- *Eating around:*

you are in luck: the hotel's *private* restaurant is renowned for its quality, but if you prefer dining out, then you are equally perfectly located. Alain Ducasse's techno-gastronomic 59 *59 avenue Raymond-Poincaré, 01.47.27.59.59* immediately comes to mind, but also for tasty, astute and irresistibly on-the-up Seize au seize *16 avenue Bugeaud, 01.56.28.16.16* or, not far away, the opulently Italian Pascal Fayet's Sormani *4 rue du Général-Lanzerac, 01.43.80.13.91*. If you are more inclined towards classicism and irreproachable technique, don't hesitate to reserve at Jamin *32 rue Longchamp, 01.45.53.00.07* whose chef, Benoit Guichard, was trained by Joël Robuchon. But the restaurant most deserving of attention is undoubtedly Ormes *8 rue Chapu, 01.46.47.83.98*. The waiting list to eat at L'Astrance *4 rue Beethoven, 01.40.50.84.40* is unfortunately far too long for short-term visitors to the city. Why? Because it is the best restaurant in the arrondissement.

- *The Golden Triangle:*

on avenue Victor-Hugo: Holland & Holland, Hobbs, Céline, Apostrophe, Yves Saint Laurent… and also Gap and Zara. Lemaire et la Boutique 22 for their excellent cigars and Point à la ligne to light up your table!

- *Soul food:*

everything on the same square: le musée de la Marine *at n°. 17*, le musée de l'Homme *at the same address*, le théâtre de Chaillot *at n°. 1*…

- *Croissants and press:*

Two excellent bakers are on avenue Victor-Hugo: Bechu *at n°. 118* and Carton *at n°. 150*. Newsstands just in front.

SAINT-JAMES PARIS

43 AVENUE BUGEAUD 75016 PARIS

TEL.: +33 (1) 44 05 81 81
FAX: +33 (1) 44 05 81 82

E-MAIL RESERVATIONS:
contact@saint-james-paris.com
Website: www.saint-james-paris.com

- *Rooms from 380 to 460 dollars,*
  suites from 500 to 780 dollars
  - *24-hour room service* -
  Baby-sitting
  - *Bar* - *Restaurant* -
  Sauna - *Jacuzzi*
  - *Health club* - *Parking*

Reading matter

The library bar is so sumptuous one could almost forget
to go and have dinner. But the 12,000 volumes lining
the walls, mostly devoted to law and algebra, make
pretty stodgy food for thought.

Upstairs

On the third floor, one reaches one's rooms via indoor
terraces reminiscent of the Hospices de Beaune.

Nikita

You may remember this staircase in Luc Besson's movie
Nikita. He transformed the hotel into the Russian
embassy, into which Anne Parillaud sneaked one
night in search of vital documents.

Bathrooms

The beautiful bathrooms and tall narrow doorways are
vestiges of Andrée Putman's initial remodeling of the
Saint James, later complemented by Philippe Hurel.

SQUARE

*The egoistic pleasure
of the atypical*

It was one of those foibles of late twentieth-century Parisian property development: the vacant lot next door to France's state media epicenter, La Maison de la Radio. For years it had languished in the eighties, one of the capital's choicest chunks of real estate, on which, it had been assumed, would be built a worthy counterpart, a match for its august, monolithic neighbor – not the squat, four-floor affair that eventually went up instead. The hotel, brainchild of its owner and designer, the restaurant owner Patrick Derderian, had been a long time in the making. There had been setbacks, delays, postponements, planning permission problems and banking difficulties (the project nearly cost Derderian his financial skin). But nothing could stop him. Le Square was to be the flagship of the Derderian fleet (the Framboisier chain of patisseries, the Amanguier and O'Poivrier restaurant chains and fashionable venues such as the Bermuda Onion, Café Mosaic and Zebra Square). But our man had other all-consuming passions: his collection of works in glass, of course, but above all an obsession with drawing and design. In trains, planes, everywhere he goes he fills sketchpad after sketchpad. Everything in his restaurants, bars and shops is drawn by him (the wave is a recurrent theme). A trip to Dallas redoubled his

enthusiasm for architecture. With Le Square's two architects, Roger Tallibert (exterior) and François-Xavier Evellin (interior), he threw himself headlong into the painstaking conception of every last detail of his magnificent new vessel in green Indian marble. From the foundations up, one of the hotel's guiding principles –to conceal the sophisticated technology underpinning it– was there in evidence. The concrete walls of the underground car park already had tailor-made niches in them to house the recessed lighting.

In the rooms the air conditioning is hidden behind the ceiling moldings and the fire sprinklers are recessed. The governing idea behind this small luxury hotel (only 22 rooms) was to create a peaceful, intimate atmosphere. Behind the rosewood door of each room a delicate, feminine world designed by Coralie Hallard (Nobilis Fontan) awaits you, its discreet details, stripes and streaks echoing the hotel's overall design rhythms. Everything emphasizes the hotel's intimate dimension: the lights have dimmers, the baths are sunk into the floor (you can sit on the edge), the belt of the dressing gowns is sewn on at the back for easier use. But don't go thinking that Le Square is the product of one man's manic obsession with detail. The hotel's all-pervasive technology is merely one discreet component of an overall architectural and design scheme. Its leitmotif, the line, is celebrated everywhere one looks, in the 18-meter-high central atrium, with its superb prow-shaped staircase (the best view is from the Lounge Bar on Level 1) and large slate reception table; in the rugs and carpets by Christian Duc and the door handles and banisters by Eric Schmitts.

Le Square very soon became a celebrity hideout, pied-à-terre even. Why? one wonders. What more could this atypical designer hotel have to offer than the Paris palaces? Its laid-back discreetness, a certain reserved attitude vis-à-vis the capital, yes, definitely, but also its painstaking modesty and dogged insistence on comfort and complete calm, on creating a cocooned atmosphere. On arrival at Le Square, one shakes off the city and its excesses. No grande gastronomie in the Zebra Square restaurant, no hodgepodge of culinary delights, simply a menu in the spirit of the time, nonchalant almost, composed of no-fuss yet precision-made dishes. Yet with a 2,000-bottle wine list. Here again, the line is omnipresent. The restaurant's three levels are linked by a black-and-white mosaic carpet; on the walls, zebra stripes and other linear motifs, and a phrase by Voltaire: "He who gives pleasures has pleasure." The clientele? Active media people, many of them familiar talking heads from France's state media center next door. Later, in the wee small hours, the Lounge Bar is popular with actors and night owls.

But time now to go up to your room. The elevator is called automatically by a presence detector. Your room, n°. 3, known as the "Rotunda," is the most sought after, but every bit as much meticulous care and thought has been put into each of the other 21. Le Square has never set out to dazzle and has no intention of resting on its laurels either. Long-lasting relationships are those that are constantly cultivated, by a considerate thought here, a last-minute helping hand there – the bathroom mirrors, for instance, are equipped with an anti-steam device; and the car in which you speed discreetly out of the city to the airport has no gaudy hotel logo, shield or gold gothic lettering on it. Therein lies the charm, the art of Le Square: in its self-effacement, in the thoughts it spares for you.

à deux pas…

- *Food:*

the hotel's designer brasserie, Zebra Square, is an impeccably orchestrated performance, but anything in at least the same league is a taxi trip away. Alain Ducasse's techno-gastronomic *59 avenue Raymond-Poincaré, 01.47.27.59.59* first of all, but also the tasty, ingenious and irresistibly on-the-up Seize au seize *16 avenue Bugeaud, 01.56.28.16.16* or, not far away, the opulently Italian Sormani *4 rue du Général-Lanzerac, 01.43.80.13.91*. If your inclination is towards classicism and irreproachable culinary technique, don't hesitate to reserve at Jamin *32 rue de Longchamp, 01.45.53.00.07* whose chef, Benoit Guichard, was trained by Joël Robuchon. But the restaurant most deserving of your attention is undoubtedly Ormes *8 rue Chapu, 01.46.47.83.98*. Meanwhile, the waiting list to eat at L'Astrance *4 rue Beethoven, 01.40.50.84.40* remains unfortunately far too long for visitors to the city. But it is quite simply the best restaurant in the arrondissement.

- *Lingerie:*

Chez Women Secret *56 rue de Passy*.

- *Soul food:*

musée de l'homme *17 place du Trocadéro*, Balzac's home *47 rue Raynouard*, musée d'Art moderne *11 avenue du président-Wilson*, musée national des Arts asiatiques-Guimet *6 place d'Iena*…

- *Café, croissants, paper:*

you can breakfast at the brasseries on the intersection, place Ader. There are newsstands close by.

SQUARE

3 RUE BOULAINVILLIERS 75016 PARIS

TEL.: +33 (1) 44 14 91 90
FAX: +33 (1) 44 14 91 99

E-MAIL RESERVATIONS:
hotel.square@wanadoo.fr
Website: www.hotelsquare.com

- *Rooms from 240 to 300 dollars,*
  suites from 385 to 450 dollars,
  22 rooms and suites
- *Zebra Square Café and restaurant*
- *Conference rooms and lounge*
  (with a movie screen,
  small stage and sound system)
- *Fitness club • Parking*

Bloc

Square's interior designer is a devil for detail: here, the
washbasin was carved out of solid marble, with the
visible plumbing in chrome and a sunken bath.

Restaurant

The advantage of Square is you have everything
at your fingertips: a modern brasserie patronized by
personalities from the neighboring French state TV
and radio center and a club lounge in vogue
with Paris's trendy set.

Design

Everywhere you look, the eye alights on little designer
touches: here the undulating door echoing the
hotel's leitmotif, the wave, and the room
number projected on the threshold.

Alone at last

After a long day, soak up the gently feminine
atmosphere of Coralic Hallard's room decor playing
on Square's all-pervasive zebra stripe motif.

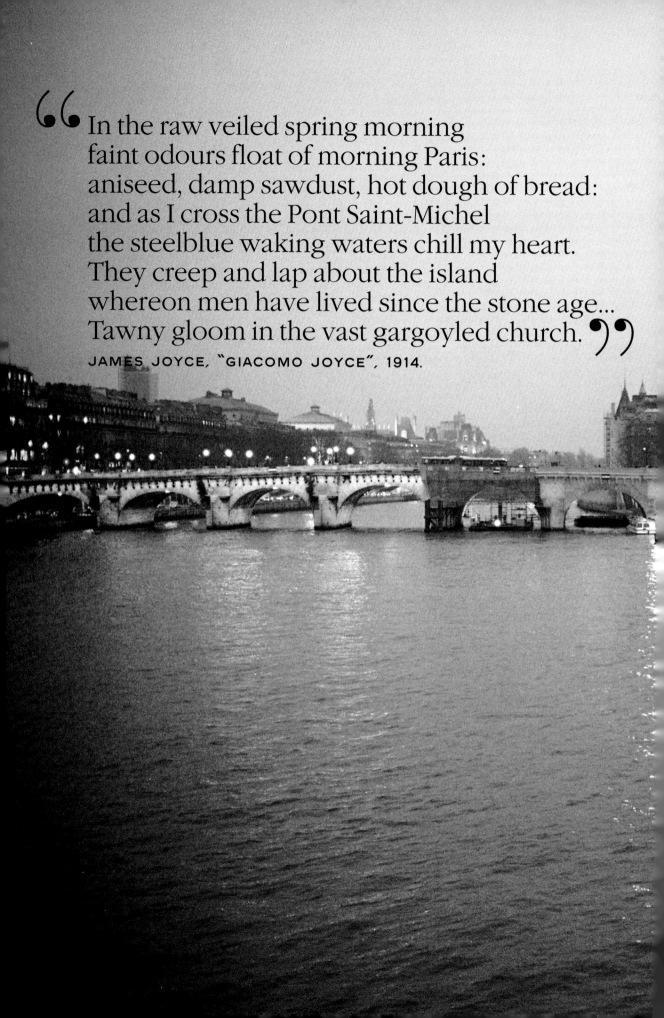

" In the raw veiled spring morning
faint odours float of morning Paris:
aniseed, damp sawdust, hot dough of bread:
and as I cross the Pont Saint-Michel
the steelblue waking waters chill my heart.
They creep and lap about the island
whereon men have lived since the stone age...
Tawny gloom in the vast gargoyled church. "

JAMES JOYCE, "GIACOMO JOYCE", 1914.

HÔTEL

—◆—

The incredible invisible hotel

"I'm dying as I have lived... beyond my means."
Oscar Wilde

No doorman, no bellboy, no name outside. You could pass Hôtel without even knowing it was there, as easily as one can a stroke of luck, an unseen opportunity. But don't worry, Hôtel doesn't mind. Hôtel is accustomed to being invisible. Continue on your way unawares.

Nor when you enter this magical hotel for the first time, when you first set foot in the small central lobby, will you immediately notice what is above you. You will merely have a strange sensation, a feeling that something is there... until finally you look up and see it: the majestic cylindrical space soaring upward. You can't quite believe your eyes. It's like being inside a hollow Trajan's column – with landings, onto which give rooms.

Hôtel began life in 1815 as the Hôtel d'Allemagne, then changed its name in 1870 to the (equally bland) Hôtel d'Alsace. Decades, eras came and went: the motorcar, the telephone, jazz, the airplane, cinema, two world wars, rock and roll, television, the Beatles. The whole twentieth century could well have passed the hotel by if a textile magnate hadn't felt sad and lonely one day in Geneva in the 1960s.

The Frenchman Edmond Dreyfus, having amassed his famed textile fortune, had done as one does —moved to Switzerland— and then, as one does, realized money isn't everything. The only thing that would make the morose multimillionaire feel better would be to see a certain tall, handsome young man again. Upon which his sister hopped into a plane to Paris and returned three days later with the missing person, the artist, model and

actor Guy-Louis Duboucheron. And of course Edmond immediately recovered his long-lost joie de vivre and expressed his boundless gratitude by heaping gifts on Guy-Louis and his nine brothers and sisters. Legend has it that when Guy-Louis's sisters marveled at the new coat their brother appeared in one day, six identical ones were sent round by courier that night. But the fairy tale doesn't end there. Edmond and Guy-Louis also fell in love with No. 1 rue des Beaux-Arts and, with the help of the architect Robin Westbrook, radically transformed the hotel, keeping the extraordinary staircase in the central atrium.

The rest is history. Oscar Wilde's room (16, during the Hôtel d'Alsace period) was recreated exactly as it was. He died at the hotel, leaving behind a huge unpaid bill and, in a final moment of lucidity, left us with these words: "I am dying as I have lived... beyond my means." Room 36 is Mistinguett's. The singer and dancer never lived there, but all the 1920s art deco furniture belonged to her, including the bed. The room's mirror-covered furniture was designed by Jean-Gabriel Domergue for the Dolly Sisters. Room 34 is entirely in leopard skin. Rooms 14 and 48 are tiny but the most sought after. The superb 26, once called the Rotunda, now the Marco Polo Room, was Claudia Cardinale's favorite. One day, when asked why she was sitting in the switchboard operator's chair downstairs, she replied, "The poor girl was hungry. I told her to go and have lunch!" "But Madame Cardinale!" "What do you think I did before I became an actress?" The phone rang and she answered, "Hôtel, bonsouaaaar...," quite possibly to someone as famous as herself.

Bianca Jagger stayed in the garden apartment during her pregnancy. She initially intended to stay only ten days but remained six months, creating a back-up in the reservation book as long as the traffic jam caused by the arrival of the Rolling Stones' thirteen limousines. One morning, Yves Dantoing, L'Hôtel's "Mr. Memory" recounts, Bianca J. called reception and asked for a yellow Rolls for 2 p.m. The hotel phoned every-where and finally located one. The only trouble was it wouldn't be available until 3 p.m. At which point, Bianca breezed into the lobby in a superb canary yellow suit. Bemused by the pandemonium her request had unleashed, she said, "But, really, Yves, you shouldn't have gone to all that trouble. There's one right here," and took a yellow rose from the vase on the reception desk. Robert de Niro always demanded the suite looking out over the Saint-Germain rooftops. Elizabeth Taylor, when she arrived in the hotel's largest suite, was enchanted and said, "This is perfect for my luggage, but where's my suite?"

Hôtel is undoubtedly the most discreet of the famous Paris hotels. No numbers on the rooms and, of course, no visitors' book. If there were the names would be dazzling: Ava Gardner, Princess Grace of Monaco, Rudolph Nureyev, David Bowie, Alice Cooper, the Aga Khan, Paul McCartney... But Hôtel also has its star maids. The famous fourth-floor maid, Dedée, for instance. She was capable of waiting up until four o'clock in the morning to welcome a guest with a beaming smile and something to eat. She often did her clients' shopping herself, tracking down their every desire (sweet chestnut honey, chamomile soap). It should be said that Hôtel has a reputation for the tips left by guests.

A short while ago, Hôtel was taken over by Jean-Paul and Elisabeth Besnard, and its kitsch heritage done away with by interior designer Jacques Garcia. After which certain famous clients never returned (only to make way for others). Hôtel didn't even bat an eyelid. Why should it? The constant flow of famous visitors dates back to the seventeenth century, when the licentious Queen Margot had her "love pavilion" on the very same site.

à deux pas…

- *Eating around:*

the hotel has an extremely pleasant restaurant spurred on by a young and ambitious chef but the district also has some interesting culinary experiences in store: the Emporio Armani Caffé *149 boulevard Saint-Germain, 01.45.48.62.15* for instance, the excellent italian restaurant Cherche-Midi *22 rue du Cherche-Midi, 01.45.48.27.44* and the old-worldly Allard *41 rue Saint-André-des-Arts, 01.43.26.48.23*, with its fine roast chicken, isn't bad either. But if you're looking for a more offbeat bistro experience, opt for Le Petit Saint Pourçain *10bis rue Servandoni, 01.43.54.93.63*. Meanwhile, Lipp remains its old magnetic and powerfully evocative self *151 boulevard Saint-Germain, 01.45.48.53.91*.

- *Boutique therapy:*

Saint-Germain is there at your fingertips: rue de Seine with its galeries such as the very nice galerie Doria, rue Bonaparte and rue du Cherche-Midi, and shops such as Vanessa Bruno *25 rue Saint-Sulpice*; Onward, Hobbs, Armani, Sonia Rykiel and Shu Uemura on boulevard Saint-Germain; Louis Vuitton *next to the Deux-Magots Café*; Irié *8 rue Pré-aux-Clercs*; David Vincent *7 rue Suger*.

- *Ear, nose and throat:*

there is a good pharmacy on Saint-Germain square.

- *Brain food:*

bibliophiles need go no further: Hôtel is in the heart of the Left Bank's booksellerland. Rare, antiquarian, foreign or hot off the press, seek out that long- sought volume or just while away the day browsing…

- *Café, croissants, papers:*

catch up on the press at the excellent newsstand on Boulevard Saint-Germain, then breakfast at Flore or Deux-Magots.

HÔTEL

13 RUE DES BEAUX-ARTS 75006 PARIS

TEL.: +33 (1) 44 41 99 00
FAX: +33 (1) 43 25 64 81

E-MAIL RESERVATION:
reservation@l-hotel.com
Website: www.l-hotel.com

- *Double rooms from 275
to 625 dollars, suites from 625
to 725 dollars, 16 rooms,
3 suites and 1 flat*
- *Le Bélier restaurant •
Swimming-pool*
- *Hammam*

Vertigo
You walk into the lobby for the first time, unsuspecting.
Then you look up at the magnificent sight soaring
above you…

The Garcia touch
The general consensus is that designer Jacques Garcia,
who recently remodeled Hôtel, has left the hotel's
soul largely intact, as here in the library lounge.

Worlds
Each room is a world unto itself (here, by Pierre Loti),
and this is one of the Hôtel's delights: passing from one
climate or continent to another…

Bathrooms
Hôtel's bathrooms, with their baths set in alcoves
or cocooned in drapes, often have a nest-like
feel about them.

BEL-AMI

———— ◆ ————

That friend of yours in Saint-Germain-des-Prés

There are those hotels one sometimes considers almost as a friend, always there for you, ever ready to lend a sympathetic ear. Bel-Ami could well be that friend waiting for you in Saint-Germain-des-Prés. A lighthearted, casual, almost fatuous friend – just those qualities that at certain moments in life can metamorphose into cardinal virtues. During those stays, for instance, which seem to be cloaked in grace, in a delicious fleeting magic, when one hardly wants even to be greeted on entering, let alone asked one's room number...

You've reserved 114. The room has an informal, unaffected elegance in raw ochre, earth and olive-green tones. The TV? – concealed behind foldaway doors in the wenge hardwood wardrobe. You lie down on the bed and steal one of those brief winter naps from which one wakes with one's energy completely restored. Your face has a newfound calm about it. When you wake night is already falling. Paris is entering its indigo hour, and your 7 p.m. rendezvous draws closer. Café de Flore, right-hand terrace. When you reserved the table you were asked for a name and for a moment you were tempted to echo Albert Camus, who, to retain his anonymity in certain cafés, called himself Mr. Terrace. Instead, you did as one often does in Paris, you merely gave your first name.

Everything has been perfectly, beautifully planned. All that remains for you to do now is savor what will undoubtedly be the most delectable moment of your rendezvous: from the bed, parting the curtains slightly, you have a perfect voyeur's view of the café terrace at the end of rue Saint-Benoît, on the corner of Boulevard Saint-Germain. On the boulevard, the rhythmic swell of passers-by ebbs and flows. 6:45...

Peaceful rue Saint-Benoît was once called rue des Egouts – Sewer Street. It led to the

Saint-Germain monastery, which in the late fourteenth century Pope Alexandre III entered through a gateway situated in the hotel lobby. The monastery's walls have long since disappeared, but the two angels carved on the hotel's facade attest to the site's ecclesiastical past. They also lent their name to the tiny nearby street off rue Saint-Benoît: Impasse des Deux Anges – Two Angels' Path.

Five minutes to go. You savor every second of these final mouth-watering minutes of waiting, every instant in their inexorable escalation. Much has been written about such moments and, of course, their quasi-obligatory and oh-so-Parisian companion: unpunctuality, always ready to turn it all sour. Five past seven... Then, just as you are about to swallow the bitter pill – that fleeting, furtive apparition your were waiting for. Commotion, emotion... and suddenly there you are basking in the wonderful aftermath, sipping the cream and dark bitterness of a café viennois, talking, talking until the two of you find yourselves, as always, first in the bookshop La Hune, just opposite, then in the newsstand outside. Your evening prayer was answered. The church bells are ringing for Vespers as you return to your friend in the rue Saint-Benoît, where you sink, eyes full of stars, mouth full of flowers, into waiting sheets.

Later, outside again, the Saint-Germain evening impishly sticks its tongue out at you

—"No more words now"— as you make your way over to rue des Canettes for that long-awaited pizza at Chez Bartolo (where, you note, you have paper table napkins and the regulars linen ones). But you soon return to rue Saint-Benoît, which, so the story goes, locals used to call Zigzag Street because of the way drunken hansom-cab drivers used to drive up it.

In the eighteenth century the hotel building was taken over by the State printing works, and a printing press still exists along the street, on a different site. The hotel, for a while called the Hôtel Alliance, had a succession of owners before its complete makeover by the hotel renovation specialist Grace Leo-Andrieu (the Guanahani on St. Barts; the Clarence, Dublin; and the Montalembert and Lancaster in Paris). The target clientele: young, busy globetrotters attuned to the latest design trends and technology. A young woman sits at one of the two computers for guests' use in the lobby. A couple passes furtively, books under their arms. It is their insouciance, a certain gay, cheerful, lightheartedness that catches your attention rather than their faces. Hôtel Bel-Ami, room 114.

à deux pas...

- *Left Bank cuisine:*

the restaurants in the immediate vicinity are all fairly predictable except for Gilles Choukroum's Café des Délices *87 rue d'Assas, 01.43.54.70.00,* with its disconcerting dishes such as foie gras crumble and shrimps with olives and coriander, and the teppanyaki hotplate cuisine of the neo-Japanese Azabu *3 rue Mazet, 01.46.33.72.05.* There is also Les Bookinistes *53 quai des Grands-Augustins, 01.43.25.45.94,* a contemporary-style bistro with its brilliant new annex, Ze Kitchen Galérie *4 rue des Grands-Augustins, 01.44.32.00.32.*
And while you're in the area, try Epi Dupin at 11 rue Dupin *01.42.22.64.56.* For other kinds of restaurants, consult the Lutetia, Montalembert and Hôtel pages.

- *Shopping around:*

for eau de toilette and perfumed candles, Diptyque *34 bd Saint-Germain.*
For those whose stay in Florence was too short, Santa Maria Novella Pharmacy products can be procured at Amin Kader *2 rue Cuisarde.* Frédéric Malle *37 rue de Grenelle* is another perfumer well worth visiting, and of course Jean Laporte *84bis rue de Grenelle,* master perfumer and glove maker, is just a little further on.

- *Advice, ointments, creams:*

the Elalouf pharmacy *26 rue du Four.*

- *The next day:*

breakfast at Café de la Mairie, a writers' hangout on Place Saint-Sulpice, or even better, the ultra-private Aoki Sadahuru *35 rue de Vaugirard, 01 45 44 48 90.* There's a newsstand on that same Saint-Sulpice square.

BEL-AMI

7-11 RUE SAINT-BENOÎT 75006 PARIS

TEL.: +33 (1) 42 61 53 53
FAX: +33 (1) 49 27 09 33

E-MAIL RESERVATIONS:
contact@hotel-bel-ami.com
Website: www.hotel-bel-ami.com

- *Rooms from 295 to 420 dollars,*
  suites from 515 dollars,
  125 rooms and 2 suites
  - *Expresso bar*
  - *Funky bar*
- *Conference rooms*

Decor
Bel-Ami's charm is undoubtedly its carefree, light-hearted spirit. The aim, as here in the cafeteria, was to create a playful atmosphere; the end-product is a hotel bubbling with mischievous charm.

Cafeteria
The hotel's self-service restaurant has become one of Paris's trendiest eating places, quite simply because the food is light and the atmosphere airy.

Bathrooms
Clearly, Bel-Ami envisioned the bathroom not as an insipid washing place but as a room with its own presence and character.

Recharging
When tiredness catches up with you, the room takes over, its restful forms and atmosphere weaving that deliciously light, restful Bel-Ami climate.

VILLA SAINT-GERMAIN

After the storm

When La Villa opened in Saint-Germain des Prés in 1989, tout Paris had eyes only for her. The hotel's young interior designer, Marie-Christine Dorner (a pupil of Philippe Starck), had succeeded in limpidly encapsulating a whole new fin-de-siècle intimacy in her cloud-shaped plaster ceiling lights, stretched taffeta, elegant knots emphasizing the bed corners and metal bobbin lamps inset into the pouf-like padded-leather bed canopies. The dressing tables-cum-desks were full of secret places, and in the bathrooms, with their vast washbasins in sand-blasted glass, matching sliding doors enabled the room's entrance hall and large wardrobe to be annexed as an attendant dressing room. She also designed a limited-edition line of fourteen pieces of furniture for the hotel, ranging from a pedestal table for the bar to a breakfast table. And each room had a devilishly rolled sheet-metal door handle, and the room number was projected in light onto the carpet outside the door (one of the features that remains).

The hotel's jazz club became a regular venue for foreign musicians on tour. Along with a pack of other journalists, I once interviewed the composer Ryuichi Sakamoto there. Realizing that his powerful, chameleon-like music, flowing as effortlessly as lava, was totally in tune with the hotel, I had the idea that its acoustic atmosphere might easily be incorporated into it. I sent Marie-Christine a selection of his pieces on a cassette.

And never received a reply.

La Villa cut a fine figure. The asymmetrical gangways leading away to the jazz club or the rooms had an authentic feeling to them. The only problem was that design prodigies have a tendency to rapidly grow old, to only rarely outlive their decade. The chambermaids soon got fed up laboring with the bed knots, with endeavoring to clean the impossible-to-clean sand-blasted glass washbasins and doors. Vacuum cleaners went their heedless way chipping paint, the taffeta wilted, the modernism of the ceiling clouds began to look a little tired. Finally, the patience of the banks ran out, and the hotel was sold.

As new management always does, it ran its eye mercilessly over everything and decided that nothing was sacred. The only thing that might have saved the Dorner Villa would have been a sudden acceleration of the fashion cycle, an overnight swing back to the nineties. Instead, it was decided to give the empress a new set of clothes. Is it too late now to revisit her, you may be wondering? No, but when you do, remember that the Villa was once a cult hotel, that you're entering a living legend, one of the first —if not the first— of the designer hotels to take such daring risks.

Yes, the Villa lives on. A different, more sensible Villa now after her makeover by Jean-Philippe Nuel, who maintains that "hotels are a field of expression with little margin for error. Interior design, like fashion, has become a consumer product and, as such, is permanently

subjected to the increasingly rapid succession of trends and tendencies. Either a hotel has a clearly demarcated fashion image (and must therefore regularly change its decor to keep abreast of tendencies), or, as I believe, the decor must draw on profounder, more deep-rooted trends, ones that enable investment to be recouped and don't date too rapidly." The modernity of today's Villa, therefore, is soft-spoken,

withdrawn almost. The rooms have been given a certain Saint-Germain je ne sais quoi, the ceilings have been cleared of yesterday's clouds. Fashion is kept at arm's length here.

à deux pas…

- *Eating out:*
the teppanyaki hotplate cuisine of the neo-Japanese Azabu *3 rue Mazet, 01.46.33.72.05*; there is also Les Bookinistes *53 quai des Grands-Augustins, 01.43.25.45.94*, a contemporary-style bistrot; the Café Parisien's *1 rue d'Assas, 01.45.44.41.44* hamburgers are delicious ; and don't forget le Voltaire *27 quai Voltaire, 01.42.61.17.49*.

- *Shopping around:*
fashionistas have all the great shoemakers at their fingertips on rue de Grenelle, rue du Cherche-Midi and rue du Dragon: *Christian Louboutin, Guido Pasquali, Hogan, Stéphane Kelian, Patrick Cox, Jean-Baptiste Rautureau, Rossetti, Sergio Rossi…* For fresh garden roses all year long, go to Au nom de la rose *50 rue du Cherche-Midi*, then test the new white truffles macaroons at Pierre Hermé *72 rue Bonaparte*.

- *Ear, nose and throat:*
there is a good pharmacy at Saint Germain and also Zagorski *6 rue Jacob*, which has an excellent product range: *orchid bubble bath*. Otherwise, there is always Elalouf *26 rue du Four* for its advice, ointments and creams.

- *Soul food:*
it is the area of the Seine bookshops, without omitting all the cinemas.

- *Café, croissants, press:*
delicious breakfasts at la Palette *43 rue de Seine, 01.43.26.68.15*.

VILLA SAINT-GERMAIN

29 RUE JACOB 75006 PARIS

TEL.: +33 (1) 43 26 60 00
FAX: +33 (1) 46 34 63 63

E-MAIL RESERVATIONS:
hotel@villa-saintgermain.com
Website: www.villa-saintgermain.com

- *Rooms from 250
to 350 dollars,
suites from 465 dollars,
31 rooms and suites*
- *Bar* -
24-hour room service
- *Conference room* -
Internet

Decor

The rooms were recently redesigned by Jean-Philippe Nuel, who replaced their once ultra-fashionable but now dated decor with a more durable modernity.

Life

The hotel's acclaimed jazz club downstairs has been transformed by the Villa's new owners into a dining room, which one reaches by this elegantly curved staircase.

Details

Opened in 1989, the Villa was originally designed by Marie Christine Dorner, many of whose little touches – such as the room numbers projected on the floor – have survived.

Bathrooms

The bathrooms fully reflect the hotel's choice of a more classical (and practical) modernity, although certain rooms have kept their original sand-blasted glass washbasins.

LUTETIA

❖

The hotel stratosphere

All on its own on the Left Bank, out on a limb down there at Sèvres-Babylone. And perfectly fine right where she is, thank you, as content as ever to gaze regally out across the indolent square at that other stately stand-alone queen of the Left Bank, the Bon Marché department store. And besides, above the bustle on Boulevard Raspail, over the sea of rooftops, there is that superb view of the Eiffel Tower.

Those out with their butterfly nets in search of that elusive Rive Gauche ésprit only have to sit at the back of the lobby and stake out the eternally revolving door. There is a perpetual effervescence at the Lutetia. It's better than watching a film: people coming and going with their luggage and sunglasses, caught in travel's precarious liminal moments, when everything seems to hang in the balance. Filmic instants of transition, snapshots in life's eternal cinéma vérité – dissolve from one country to another, cut from an escalator at the airport to the revolving door of the hotel. Like the stopper of a perfume bottle, the Lutetia lobby says it all.

From your vantage point, you watch the mirror to the right of the revolving door. You observe a woman give herself the once-over, another adjust her décolleté, another steal a glance at her profile, all of them not only unaware that you are watching them but also that someone else may be too – from the manager's office behind the two-way mirror. But I'm sure I'll be forgiven for divulging this secret, because there are bound to be those few who, aware eyes are watching them from behind the glass, will add an extra bit of spice to the spectacle.

The two-way mirror was probably there from the beginning. The Lutetia was

inaugurated in 1910, at a time Paris had its foot hard down on the accelerator. The city was caught in the whirlwind of the Belle Epoque. The international exhibitions, new luxury hotels and couturiers were attracting people from all over the world. The Lutetia took three years to build. Famous sculptors –Léon Binet and then Belmondo (father of Jean-Paul)– were unleashed on the facade. Take a look and you'll soon see the theme running through the swirling, intertwining vine branches, grapes and vines.

There was a time when you were taking a risk standing there looking up at the ornate facade. The great French comedian Coluche, fed up with his car getting a parking ticket every morning (he insisted on parking it outside), took to throwing yogurt down on the police. The management was repeatedly questioned as to the possible source of the deluge. And of course had no idea who might possibly have done such a thing.

But before becoming a launching pad for yogurt, during the Roaring Twenties the Lutetia was a regular venue for all manner of revelry. The Russian New Year party (graced by the extravagances of Khodassevich, Kuprin, Tcherny, Nina Berberova and others) was held there annually, along with other high masses of the Paris society calendar.

On a different note, one day in 1921 a couple of newlyweds arrived to spend their wedding night at the Lutetia. The husband, a young army officer on leave, signed their names in the hotel register: M. et Mme. de Gaulle. At the sight of the lieutenant's towering height, the management immediately took the initiative of installing a specially lengthened bed in their room. But at the Lutetia—as at the Crillon and the Meurice—one should avoid talking about World War II; it would be in bad taste. One is led to understand that other occupations are far more worth talking about— the whims of the many millionaires, writers and artists who have stayed at the Lutetia, for instance. As is often the case, the choicest anecdotes often concern those who lived at the hotel year-round: André Gide and Matisse, for instance, or, more recently, César and Pierre Bergé.

Pierre Bergé always stayed in suite 608, today called the Opéra Suite, a suite I have fantasized about for years. It was the elegant somberness of its wall-to-wall wood paneling and Empire-green wall hangings that I found so breathtaking—and, of course, its splendid view of Paris and utter peace (the walls were soundproofed with lining of lead). The suite even had its own dining room. For years, I religiously saved

up to spend just one night there. Only to discover, when I visited the Lutetia to research this book, that the wall hangings had been changed, the wood paneling lightened up and the dining room converted into a bedroom. The suite had been literally stripped of its soul. The moral of the story is clear: live for today not tomorrow. Or should I now set my heart on the literary suite (606), with its plum and chocolate tones? Or perhaps the Eiffel Suite on the top floor, with its two rotunda-shaped terraces and wooden staircase leading up to the purple-and-honey-tinted bedroom. The bathroom, inspired by the architecture of Gustave Eiffel, has a circular bath from which one can admire his masterpiece.

Another of the Lutetia's supreme pleasures is the Ernest Bar, which doesn't get fully under way until late evening, when its enormous purple armchairs fill up with a lively, captivating set of night owls, or diners discussing their meal at the Lutetia's gourmet restaurant, Paris. Or you can retire to the bar's cigar lounge, a haven for Havana aficionados. At lunchtime one occasionally has the place to oneself, to sit embalmed in velvet solitude and smile.

à deux pas...

- *Eating around:*
the Lutetia's renowned gourmet restaurant "Paris" has a Michelin star, but you can also try Hélène Darroze's modernized southwestern French provincial cooking *4 rue d'Assas, 01.42.22.00.11* or Alain Passard's Arpège *84 rue de Varenne, 01.45.51.47.33*, famous for its vegetable-oriented cuisine. But there are also more everyday options such as Bamboche *15 rue de Babylone, 01.45.49.14.40*, or the refreshing Fontaines de Mars *129 rue Saint-Dominique, 01.47.05.46.44*. Even better, Christian Constant's Violon d'Ingres *135 rue Saint-Dominique, 01.45.55.15.05*. Or you could also try the excellent wines and cuisine at Vin sur Vin *20 rue de Montessuy, 01.47.05.14.20* and, in the same street, Le Bon Accueil *n°. 14, 01.47.05.46.11*, with its magical view of the Eiffel Tower when you come out.

- *Left Bank shopping:*
you have the Bon Marché department store, with its Grande Epicerie food hall opposite the hotel, *22 rue de Sèvres,* but also the whole of the formidable Saint-Germain shopping district at your fingertips. Highlights are rue du Cherche-Midi: *Eres, Poilâne, Robert Clergerie...*, APC *3-4 rue de Fleurus,* Paul Smith *22 bd Raspail* and Miu Miu *16 rue de Grenelle*.

- *Skin concerns:*
Doctor Hauschka products rose face mask, quince cream, etc. at 17 rue de Sèvres, regular clients: Jerry Hall, Madonna, Jack Nicholson, Julia Roberts...

- *Brain food:*
the musée Rodin *77 rue de Varenne* and the Musée d'Orsay *62 rue de Lille*.

- *Lingerie:*
Sabbia Rosa *71 rue des Saint-Pères* and Vanina Vesperini *60 rue des Saints-Pères*.

- *The morning after:*
take a walk down rue de Cherche-Midi and drop in at Poilâne *at n°.8*, then pick your café at the next intersection.

Nest

Rustic Adornments of Taste for homes

2300 Fillmore St.
San Francisco Ca
94115

415 292-6199

Sold to:

cash   credit   check

DATE: 2/24/0

Store Craft

5420

LUTETIA

45 BOULEVARD RASPAIL 75007 PARIS

TEL.: +33 (1) 49 54 46 46
FAX: +33 (1) 49 54 46 00

E-MAIL RESERVATIONS:
lutetia-paris@lutetia-paris.com
Website: www.lutetia-paris.com

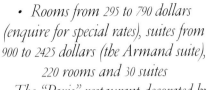

- *Rooms from 295 to 790 dollars (enquire for special rates), suites from 900 to 2425 dollars (the Armand suite), 220 rooms and 30 suites*
- *The "Paris" restaurant decorated by Sonya Rykiel*
- *The "Lutèce" piano bar*
- *Air-conditioned lounge*

Palace

High-ranking among Lutetia's delights are its ample spaces, sensuous purples and the hospitality in the bars and lounges.

Hallmark

A hotel's lobby has to say it all. Straight away, from the moment you enter, you are plunged into the inimitable Lutetia atmosphere.

Vantage point

Lutetia is an Art Deco lover's paradise. One can easily spend a day admiring the Lalique crystal chandeliers, the gray and gold stained glass up the stairways, opalescent skylights and period furniture…

Lap of luxury

The quality and comfort of a hotel's seating is often only noticed when it is excellent. Everywhere in the Lutetia, in the bars, the Ernest lounge and the "Paris" gourmet restaurant, one sits in the lap of luxury.

MONTALEMBERT

———◆———

In search of future times

There is a creased, subtly threadbare elegance about the man pacing nervously
up and down the Montalembert lobby. He lets out a sigh of exasperation and asks
whether the music could be turned down a little. The author Jean-Jacques Schuhl,
whose book Ingrid Kaven has been short-listed for the 2000 Goncourt prize, due
to be announced this afternoon, is in no mood for mood music. The receptionist
complies, no doubt mildly amused like myself. The music (a sublimely inoffensive
cocktail-lounge bossa nova) is turned respectfully down, and the Montalembert goes
back to being the Montalembert again, to doing what it does best: being chic,
modern, appealing to the mind rather than the senses. And although this is hardly
the moment, I can't resist pointing out to Jean-Jacques why hotels, restaurants and
stores sometimes raise the volume like that: to speed things up, to quicken the flow
of customers and purchases, in short, to increase turnover. The subtle annoyance of
those few extra decibels is a thinly veiled hint that the establishment has no time for
dawdlers, that it has better things to do, that perhaps—just possibly—one might not be
as welcome as one thought.

The Montalembert was one of the very first Paris hotels to "go contemporary."
Watching with amusement out of the corner of their eye, other Parisian palaces made
it known that they had better things to do, that there would be plenty of time for this
later. Meanwhile Christian Liaigre lost no time reinventing the Montalembert, swiftly
securing its reputation as one of Paris's top "design hotels"—or "boutique hotels," as
they are also sometimes called. More recently, in 2000, the efforts of previous design
teams were set aside to create "Le Nouveau Montalembert." But as its director,

Grace Leo-Andrieu (to whom we also owe the design concepts of the Bel-Ami
and the Lancaster in Paris, the Clarence in Dublin, the Château de Noirieu in
the Loire Valley, and the Cotton House Resort on Mustique, among others), explains,
"The new Montalembert is also the old Montalembert. A different, more mature
contemporary style has been integrated into the original architecture. Yet we have
gone to great lengths to preserve the spirit and the subtleties of the old
Montalembert, the one we all loved."

Gone the blue and white stripes, replaced by embroidered bed linen matching
the cinnamon-and-olive or lilac-and-gray Liberty bedspreads. In the traditional-style
rooms, the tobacco-colored fabric of the armchairs, specially designed by Canovas,
complements the cream gauze curtains. In contrast, in the modern rooms the gray
and lilac Nya Nordista fabric adds a metallic note.

The rooms are on the small side ("This is the Left Bank," is the immediate
retort). The hotel's true soul, its full-blown Parisian chic and elegance, is to be
found in the suites. Yet somehow one has the feeling that the search for a new
Montalembert state of mind is still on, that the hotel is still playing hide and seek

with itself. Long hours have been spent gazing introspectively into those mirrors.
Curves have been smoothed, lines polished, and the restaurant too has had another
facelift, the honey-colored sycamore paneling replaced by oak tinted slightly
olive green.

In the lobby, Jean-Jacques Schuhl has resumed his own inner searchings on one
of the huge padded wall seats covered with hand-woven, hazel-colored fabric.
A waiter in the Prada-style beige and gray Montalembert livery arrives with
the drink he ordered. He could well be contemplating a sequel to his 1972 novel
Rose Poussière, taking it up where it left off, with a list of the hotels Rolling Stones
guitarist Brian Jones stayed in: "The Algonquin, New York (Garbo and Mae Murray
were eating at the next table), the Tokyo Hilton, the Embassy, Brussels (the underneath of the divan was modified), the George V, Paris (on the patio where tea is taken
there are trees with artificial oranges), Hôtel du Sphinx, Lyon, the Carlton, Cannes
(the décolleté of the tee-shirt is different), Duke's Hotel, Edinburgh (a crêpe bandage
around the wrist), Hôtel de la Presse et des Messageries, Tunis, Hôtel Bijou Select,
Dakar . . . ." Ending with the phrase, "Everything here undone now."

Meanwhile, in the silence, the show goes on. The imperious dance of the material world continues: the existentialist chic of the imposing lampshades in wood and clay-colored leather by François Champsaur, the wall seats in soy-colored leather, velvet and duvet, the almond-colored walls, and the white leather armchairs with low backs and bronze feet and the settee in gray velvet in the lobby...

- *South of the Seine:*

the hotel restaurant's light, pleasant contemporary cuisine is a crowd puller but if you fancy even lighter refreshment try the Ladurée tearoom *21 rue Bonaparte*, L'heure Gourmande *22 passage Dauphine* or L'Artisan des Saveurs *72 rue du Cherche-Midi*. The food at Emporio Armani Caffé *149 boulevard Saint-Germain, 01.45.48.62.15* is just as light, provided one limits oneself to a single dish. You should also try the pleasant and tasty Mediterranean cuisine at La Bastide Odéon *7 rue Corneille, 01.43.26.03.65* and the recently opened L'Atelier de Joël Robuchon at the Hôtel Pont-Royal.

- *Brain cells:*

the district is renowned for its art galleries, the most prestigious being Claude Bernard *7 rue des Beaux-Arts*, Isy Brachot *35 rue Guénégaud*, Yves Gastou *12 rue Bonaparte* and Adrien Maeght *42 et 46 rue du Bac*.

- *Organic market:*

rub shoulders with the chic Parisian gourmets shopping at the nearby organic market on Boulevard Raspail *Sunday mornings only*. For more addresses consult the other Left Bank hotel pages *La Villa, L'Hôtel, Lutetia, etc.*.

- *The next day:*

you'll find the international press in rue Saint-Benoît; and croissants at Pierre Hermé *72 rue Bonaparte*, or at Poilâne *8 rue du Cherche-Midi*.

MONTALEMBERT

3 RUE MONTALEMBERT 75007 PARIS

TEL.: +33 (1) 45 49 68 68
FAX: +33 (1) 45 49 69 49

E-MAIL RESERVATIONS:
welcome@hotel-montalembert.fr
Website: www.montalembert.com

- *Rooms from 315 to 475 dollars,*
  suites from 550 to 810 dollars,
  50 rooms and 6 suites
- *Restaurant*
- *24-hour room service*
- *1 conference room* • *Internet access*

Overture
A hotel sets out its wares in its lobby, which functions
like an operatic overture, stating the themes and
setting the scene for what's to come.

Eating in
The Montalembert's culinary credo is simplicity and
complicity. The restaurant seeks not to embellish:
a calm, collected cuisine is often
the most effective...

Lounging
One of the hotel's many charms is its lobby, with its
attendant lounges and intimate spaces where
one can while away the afternoon watching
comings and goings, or merely contemplating
the superb flower arrangements.

Details
The Montalembert's rooms are on the small side
("This is the Left Bank," the manager explains.),
and this is undoubtedly why so much care
has been lavished on the bathrooms.

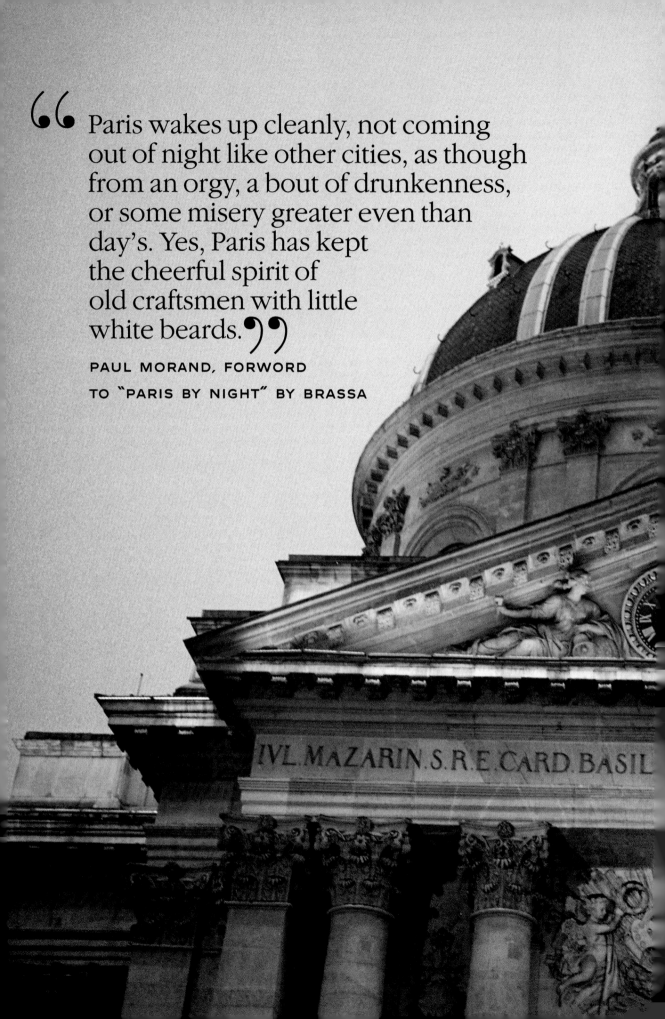

"Paris wakes up cleanly, not coming out of night like other cities, as though from an orgy, a bout of drunkenness, or some misery greater even than day's. Yes, Paris has kept the cheerful spirit of old craftsmen with little white beards."

PAUL MORAND, FORWORD
TO "PARIS BY NIGHT" BY BRASSA

"Oh! To wander Paris! Such a lovely, delectable experience! Strolling is a science, gastronomy for the eye. To walk is to merely exist, strolling is living."

HONORÉ DE BALZAC,
"PHYSIOLOGIE DU MARIAGE", 1838.

VILLA
ROYALE

The crimson lady

"To be Parisian,
is not to be born in Paris,
but to be reborn there."

SACHA GUITRY

Five a.m. Upstairs in your room, nose to the windowpane, you gaze out into the night. The teeming incandescent Pigalle night, for butterflies with fireproof wings. The strange slow motion of the curb-crawling taxis; the vermilion blaze of the Moulin Rouge, the papier-mâché windmill hypnotically going round and round... Below you, Place Pigalle already has that no man's land look about it, caught between night and day. A figure passes below, her or his light purple eyelids perfectly matching the Villa Royale's curtains. You draw them. It's time to go to bed.

Not so long ago a baroque little hotel with rococo makeup, fishnet tights and scarlet lipstick discreetly elbowed her way into the Paris hotel pantheon. There was no publicity, the word simply went around, whispered from mouth to ear, like the name of one of the brothels that once graced this part of town. And one found oneself ringing the doorbell of the Villa Royale.

A young woman opens the door and there you are in a green marble lobby, surrounded by purple settees, puce poufs and fuchsia meridennes. The woman draped on the couch, a model of immaculately disheveled chic, looks you over from behind her sunglasses. The message her carefully tousled hair, her whole look, is meant to convey somehow perfectly matches the gaudiness of the Villa Royale: "Look at me, I shot to stardom so quickly I didn't even have time to change my clothes. And wouldn't bother even if I did."

The hotel, a stone's throw away from what would become the Moulin Rouge, was inaugurated in 1879. Edith Piaf, Toulouse-Lautrec, Renoir and Degas all slept here during different eras and at different times of day. But despite its hallowed congregation of guests, the hotel refused to become a shrine. It preferred to remain

what it was, a kind of semi-sacred boudoir. Rest assured: when you step out onto the promised landings of the Villa Royale, you are not expected to kneel and kiss the carpet.

Each of the hotel's 31 rooms (21 of which give onto Place Pigalle) has a name: Coco Chanel, Serge Gainsbourg, Brigitte Bardot, Jean-Paul Gaultier, Louis Vuitton, Moulin Rouge, Cathérine Deneuve (fifth floor, on the corner looking out over Montmartre), Jean Marais – the last two are the most sought after. Today's regular guests may one day have a room named after them: Carla Bruni, Hugh Grant, Tom Ford, John Malkovich. But Pigalle must take care of its own royalty first. Michou, legendary owner of the legendary cabaret nearby, is the most recent entry into the Villa Royale hall of fame, and frequently stays in the all-blue room dedicated to him. Lie down on the Swedish blue bed, switch on the little light and gaze up at the Douarnenez blue canopy above, peppered with tiny stars. One almost expects Michou himself to pop out of some hidden door like a jack-in-the-box and shout his eternal refrain, "Wow! What a night!" But don't worry, the Villa Royale is not that kind of hotel. No need for party tricks, for cabaret razzmatazz, she bowls you

over with her sheer jaw-dropping glamour. Pink, plum or peacock-blue flowered carpets in the corridors, pink watered silk walls, multicolored Murano glass wall lamps, ornate lamp stands, lampshades fringed with pendants, drapes, canopies, crystal door handles, petite little writing desks made to measure in Romania, plasma screen in a gilded old master-style frame, remote-controlled gas fires. The passionate purple and mauve razzle-dazzle of the (not huge) rooms sweeps you off your feet. You lie there gasping, unable to get up, pinned to the floor by one of her stiletto heels.

Like the women walking the streets outside, the Villa Royale is whomever you want her to be: love nest, antechamber to a Paris netherworld, decompression chamber for the new showbiz elite, trendy, confidential. If you're looking for something a little more traditional, for a more diurnal Paris, then you only have to go a little further south. Up here on the edge of Montmartre, in the petticoat frills of Pigalle, the stars come out at night.

à deux pas…

- *Eating around:*

the hotel doesn't have a restaurant, but does offer room service, which is an option worth considering given that Montmartre is not exactly prime gourmet territory. Apart from the handful of rather pompous establishments such as Beauvilliers *52 rue Lamarck, 01.42.54.54.42*, there are one or two addresses: the adorable Italian restaurant Per Bacco *10 rue Lambert, 01.42.52.22.40* for example, or, in a younger, more tongue-in-cheek bistro vein, Café Burq *6 rue Burq, 01.42.52.81.27*, Chez Grisette *14 rue Houdon, 01.42.62.04.80* and the Sale e Pepe pizzeria *30 rue Ramey, 01.46.06.08.01*. Or, even better, reserve at Le Soleil in the Saint-Quentin flea market *109 avenue Michelet, 01.40.10.08.08*. You won't regret it.

- *Shopping:*

if you're looking for high-voltage SM-inspired lingerie, try Artistes/New Girls *19 and 69 boulevard de Clichy*. For a latex dress or something more gothic, L'Enklave *40bis rue de Douai*.

- *Body:*

there is a pharmacy on Place Pigalle.

- *Soul:*

musée de l'Érotisme, 72 boulevard de Clichy *daily from 10am to 2am*, the Moulin-Rouge *82 boulevard de Clichy, 01.46.06.00.19*.
The *"chansonniers"* of the cabaret Les Deux Ânes *100 boulebard de Clichy, 01.46.06.10.26* are back! And the tradition is to enjoy after the show seafood at Charlot, le Roi des Coquillages *81 boulevard de Clichy, 01.53.20.48.00*.

- *Morning after*:

breakfast at the brasseries on the square outside.

VILLA ROYALE

2 RUE DUPERRÉ 75009 PARIS

TEL.: +33 (1) 55 31 78 78
FAX: +33 (1) 55 31 78 70

E-MAIL RESERVATIONS:
royale@leshotelsdeparis.com
Website: www.leshotelsdeparis.com

- *Rooms from 220 dollars,
suites from 330 dollars,
34 rooms including 5 neo-baroque style suites,
(fully equipped with
plasma screen TV, jacuzzi, etc.)*
- *24-hour room service*
- *Parking*

Kitsch chic

Over-ornate lamps, pendant fringed lampshades,
multicolored Murano glass wall lamps, miniature
writing tables made to order in Hungary…
Or could the Villa Royale be merely
playing at being a hotel?

Lounging

Although the hotel's reception is hardly bigger
than a school desk, several of its rooms have
been transformed into lounges (which are
regularly reserved for interview sessions).

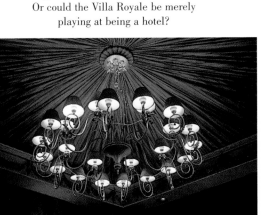

Rococo

The Villa Royale's passion for original detail is
boundless. The hotel has its own unique way of
equipping each room with cutting-edge technology
(a plasma screen in an old master-style frame),
while assuring free rein is given to the
wildest decorative fantasies.

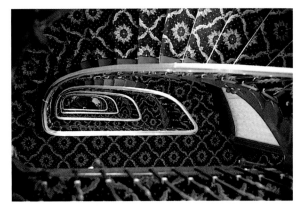

Color

Kitsch glamour is the name of the Villa Royale game:
pink, plum or peacock blue flowered carpet in the
corridors, pink watered silk walls - the rainbow
can seem dim in comparison…

INDEX

S : *shop*   C : *chef, bartender*   H : *hotel*   L : *leisure time (theater, museum...)*
P : *people*   R : *restaurant, bar, café*   D : *designer, architect*

Aga Khan P : *190*

Agnès Comar S : *90 • 102*

Alexandre III P : *196*

Algonquin H : *219*

Alice Cadolle S : *22*

Allard R : *192*

Alphonse XIII P : *37 • 38*

Amanguier R : *178*

Ambassadeurs R : *126 • 128 • 129*

Ambassy H : *219*

Ambroisie R : *78 • 80 • 142*

Ami Louis R : *22*

Amin Kader S : *198*

Angelina S : *32 • 42 • 62*

Angle du Faubourg R : *110*

Annexe des Créateurs S : *156*

Anouschka S : *156*

APC R : *214*

Apostrophe S : *102 • 166 • 174*

Aoki Sadaharu R : *198*

Argenteuil R : *62*

Armani S : *192*

Artisan des Saveurs R : *222*

Artistes/New Girls S : *234*

Astrance R : *174 • 182*

Atelier R : *222*

Attila P : *64*

Au Nom de la rose S : *206*

Audiard, Michel P : *12 • 141*

Avenue R : *90 • 102*

Azabu R : *198 • 206*

Azéma, Sabine P : *56*

Azzedine Alaïa S : *80*

Bains L : *142*

Baker, Josephine P : *92*

Bal du Moulin-Rouge L : *230 • 234*

Ballu, Isabelle D : *80*

Balzac, Honoré (de) P : *226*

Bamboche R : *214*

Bar des Théâtres R : *102*

Baretto R : *90*

Barot, Thierry C : *50*

Bartolo R : *196*

Bastide Odéon R : *222*

Beaumard, Éric C : *114 • 118 • 119*

Beauvilliers R : *234*

Bechu S : *174*

Bellucci, Monica P : *22*

Belmondo, Paul D : *211*

Benetti, Augustin P : *142*

Berberova, Nina P : *211*

Bergé, Pierre P : *212*

Berlutti S : *146*

Bermuda Onion S : *178*

Bernard, Claude D : *222*

Besnard, Jean-Paul and Elisabeth P : *190*

Besson, Luc P : *56 • 173 • 175*

Bey de Tunis P : *36*

Binet, Léon D : *211*

Blanc, Patrick D : *89 • 91*

Blason R : *22*

Bœuf sur le toit R : *138*

Bon Accueil R : *214*

Bon Marché S : *214*

Bookinistes R : *198 • 206*

Bossuet P : *74*

Boutique 22 S : *166 • 174*

Bourgogne R : *80*

Bowie, David P : *161 • 190*

Brachot, Isy D : *222*

Brando, Marlon P : *161*

Brentano's S : *14*

Brialy, Jean-Claude P : *56*

Briffard, Éric C : *166*

Brosse, Thierry (de la) C : *22*

Bulldog R : *67*

Cacharel S : *52*

Café Burq R : *234*

Café de Flore R : *192 • 195*

Café de Marly R : *22 • 62*

Café de la Mairie R : *198*

Café des Délices R : *198*

Café des Phares R : *80*

Café Mosaic R : *178*

Café Parisien R : *206*

Café Ruc R : *22*

Calvin Klein S : *102*

Campbell, Naomi P : *107*

Camus, Albert P : *195*

Cardinale, Claudia P : *188*

Carette S : *166*

Carlton H : *220*

Caron S : *102*

Carré des Feuillants R : *14 • 70*

Cartier S : *14 • 66 • 84 • 90*

Cartier, Louis-Ferdinand P : *64*

Cartland, Barbara P : *114*

Carton S : *174*

Casa Olympe R : *156*

Caves Legrand S : *52*

Céladon R : *14 • 67 • 70*

Céline S : *90 • 102 • 166 • 174*

Centre Georges-Pompidou L : *80*

César P : *212*

Champenier di Giovanni, Yolande P : *42*

Champsaur, François D : *220*

Chanel S : *22*

Charles Bosquet S : *146*

Charlot, le Roi des Coquillages R : *234*

Chaumet S : *66*

Chenets R : *67*

Cherche-Midi 22 R : *192*

Chez Catherine R : *110*

Chez Denise R : *32*

Chez Jean R : *156*

Chiberta R : *110 • 138*

Choltitz (Von) P : *36*

Choukroun, Gilles C : *198*

Christian Lacroix S : *110*

Christian Louboutin S : *206*

Christie's S : *102* • *146*

Cinq R : *166*

Cocteau, Jean P : *92*

Colette S : *22* • *110*

Colombe R : *14*

Coloré S : *166*

Coluche P : *211*

Comédie-Française L : *14* • *52* • *62*

Conran, Terence D : *145* • *146* • *147*

Conran S : *70*

Constant, Christian C : *214*

Cooper, Alice P : *190*

Cortile H : *14*

Costes, Gilbert P : *16*

Costes, Jean-Louis P : *16* • *18* • *19* • *90* • *102*

Courrèges D : *220*

Crillon H : *50*

Curtis, Tony P : *142*

Dali, Salvador P : *37*

Dalloyau R : *80* • *110*

Dantoing, Yves P : *188*

Dauphin R : *42* • *62*

David Vincent S : *192*

Debbouze, Jamel P : *16*

Debuisson, Roxane C : *126*

Degas P : *230*

Delahaye, François D : *96*

Delon, Alain P : *56*

Depp, Johnny P : *16*

Derderian, Patrick P : *178*

Deux-Magots S : *192*

Didier Ludot S : *52* • *62*

Diep R : *146*

Dietrich, Marlene P : *131* • *135*

Dior S : *90* • *102*

Diptyque S : *198*

Disney, Walt P : *161*

Dolly Sisters P : *188*

Domergue, Jean-Gabriel D : *188*

Dorner, Marie-Christine D : *200* • *202* • *207*

Dreyfus, Edmond D : *186*

Drouot-Montaigne S : *102* • *118* • *140* • *146* • *166*

Drugstore Publicis Étoile S : *166*

Duboucheron, Guy-Louis D : *186*

Duc, Christian D : *180*

Ducasse, Alain C : *22* • *90* • *96* • *102* • *103* • *146* • *166* • *174* • *182*

Duke's Hotel H : *220*

Duke's R : *32* • *67* • *70* • *71*

Dumas, Marc D : *50*

Duncan, Isadora P : *126*

Dunhill S : *14*

Dussollier, André P : *56*

Dutournier, Alain C : *70* • *14*

Dutronc, Jacques P : *44*

Duverger, Maurice P : *168*

Eiffel, Gustave P : *213*

Eisenhower P : *112*

Elalouf S : *198* • *206*

Éluard, Paul P : *6*

Élysée Palace H : *92*

Élysées des Vernet R : *166*

Emporio Armani Café R : *192* • *222*

Enklave S : *234*

Épi Dupin R : *198*

Eres S : *214*

Ermenegildo Zegna S : *14*

Espadon R : *14* • *26*

Essenine, Sergei Alexandrovitch P : *126*

Étienne Marcel R : *22* • *52*

Étoile R : *166*

Evelin, F.-Xavier D : *178*

Everett, Rupert P : *39* • *43*

Fellini, Federico P : *161*

Ferme des Mathurins R : *128*

Ferre, Gianfranco S : *156*

Field, Colin P. C : *27* • *31*

Fifi Chachnil S : *32*

Flora R : *118*

Flottes R : *14* • *42* • *128*

Fonda, Bridget P : *56*

Fontaine de Mars R : *214*

Ford, Harrison P : *142*

Foucault, Michel P : *168*

Fouquet S : *146*

Fouquet's R : *118* • *138*

Framboisiers S : *178*

France et Choiseul H : *16*

Fréchon, Éric C : *109* • *110* • *111*

Frédéric Malle S : *198*

Fred S : *66*

Frères Costes C : *102*

Funès (de), Louis P : *142*

Gabin, Jean P : *142*

Gagarine, Youri P : *92*

Gagnaire, Pierre C : *90* • *118* • *166*

Gainsbourg, Serge P : *120* • *154* • *161*

Galerie R : *102*

Galerie Doria S : *192*

Galerie du Jeu de Paume L : *62* • *128*

Galerie Vivienne S : *14*

Galeries Lafayette S : *70* • *156*

Galignani S : *42* • *62*

Gap S : *70* • *174*

Garbo, Greta P : *112*

Garcia, Jacques D : *8* • *18* • *19* • *89* • *190* • *193*

Gardner, Ava P : *161* • *190*

Gastou, Yves D : *222*

George V H : *90* • *219*

Georges (4e arr.) R : *22*

Georges (2e arr.) R : *52*

Georgette R : *156*

Gere, Richard P : *142*

Gethers, Peter P : *142*

Gide, André P : *212*

Girod, Francis P : *56*

Godard, Jean-Luc P : *161*

Golden Black R : *154* • *157*

Goyard S : *32* • *110*

Graff, François-Joseph D : *78*

Grand Café du Grand Hôtel R : *70*

Grand Hôtel Terminus H : *152*

Grand Véfour R : *70*

Granet, Roseline D : *12*

Grisette R : *234*

Grosser, Alfred P : *168*

Gucci R : *42* • *110*

Guerlain S : *32*

Guichard, Benoît C : *174* • *182*

Guido Pasquali S : *206*

Guirlande de Julie R : *80*

Guitry, Sacha P : *229*

Habitat S : *70*

Hall, Jerry P : *214*

Hallard, Coralie D : *179* • *183*

Harry's New York Bar R : *31* • *42*

Haushka S : *214*

Hédiard S : *118*

Hélène Darroze R : *214*

Hemingway Bar R : *27* • *33* • *42*

Hemingway, Ernest P : *31*

Hepburn, Katharine P : *161*

Hermès S : *42* • *110*

Hervey, Frederick P : *104*

Heure gourmande R : *222*

Hierro D : *154*

Hillman, Joël P : *112*

Hilton H : *219*

Hobbs S : *146* • *166* • *174* • *192*

Hogan S : *206*

Holland & Holland S : *174*

Horowitz, Vladimir P : *161*

Hôtel Bijou Select H : *220*

Hôtel d'Allemagne H : *186*

Hôtel d'Alsace H : *186*

Hôtel de Castellane H : *104*

Hôtel de la Presse et des Messageries H : *220*

Hôtel du Lac H : *84*

Hôtel du Sphinx H : *220*

Hugo, Victor P : *72* • *74*

Huismans, Georges P : *168*

Hurel, Philippe D : *173*

Ibu Gallery S : *62*

Irié S : *192*

Irons, Jeremy P : *56*

Isami R : *80*

Isse R : *62*

Jagger, Bianca P : *188*

Jagger, Mick P : *101*

Jamin R : *174* • *182*

Jammet, Hippolyte P : *104*

Jaulmes, Gustave-Louis D : *108* • *111*

Jean Laporte S : *198*

Jean-Baptiste Rautureau S : *206*

Jean-Paul Gaultier S : *156*

Jean-Claude Hévin S : *110*

John, Elton P : *26*

John Nollet S : *22*

Johnston, Tim C : *52*

Jones, Brian P : *112* • *219*

Joyce, James P : *184*

Jünger, Ernst P : *165*

Junku S : *62*

Juvéniles R : *52*

Karajan, Herbert (von) P : *92*

Karyo, Tchéky P : *56*

Kelly, Gene P : *112*

Kennedy, John Fitzgerald P : *26* • *92* • *161*

Kenzo S : *52*

Khodassevich P : *211*

Kinugawa R : *42* • *62*

Knizze S : *42*

Köchler, Werner P : *96*

Kouprine P : *211*

Ladies & Gentlemen S : *80*

Ladurée S : *128* • *138* • *222*

Lalique D : *215*

Lancaster, Burt P : *161*

Lancel S : *14*

Lanvin S : *110*

Lanzmann, Jacques P : *44*

Lasserre R : *138*

Laurent R : *138*

Le Calvez, Dider P : *114*

Leatham, Jeff D : *114* • *119*

Lecuiller, Patrick D : *88*

Ledoyen R : *138*

Ledoyen, Virginie P : *22*

Legendre, Philippe C : *90* • *114* • *118* • *119*

Leigh, Vivien P : *112*

Lemaire S : *116* • *174*

Lennon, John P : *112*

Leo-Andrieu, Grace D : *134* • *136* • *139* • *197* • *218*

Lescure R : *42*

Li, Jet P : *57*

Liaigre, Christian D : *216*

Lindbergh, Charles P : *92*

Lipp R : *192*

Lisch, Juste D : *152*

Lloyd, Harold P : *161*

Lollobrigida, Gina P : *163*

Loti, Pierre D : *193*

Lotti H : *14*

Louis XVI P : *51*

Lucas Carton R : *54* • *70* • *128*

Lyonnais R : *22*

Madonna P : *214*

Maeght, Adrien D : *222*

Maison-Blanche R : *102* • *146*

Maison de Balzac L : *182*

Maison du Chocolat S : *146*

Majestic H : *159*

Marais, Stéphane S : *32*

Marant, Isabel D : *80*

Marc Delacre S : *146*

Marchesi, Gualtiero C : *14*

Maria Luisa S : *22*

Mariage Frères S : *80*

Marie-Antoinette P : *51* • *135*

Marius et Janette R : *118*

Marvin, Lee P : *142*

Massaro S : *14*

Mata, Hari P : *92*

Matisse P : *212*

Mauboussin S : *66*

Maxim's R : *128*

McCartney, Paul P : *161* • *190*

Menuhin, Yehudi P : *142*

Mikula, Flora C : *118*

Mishima, Ykio P : *160*

Miss Metrot P : *25*

Mistinguett P : *188*

Miu Miu S : *214*

Monaco, Grace (de) P : *190*

Montaigne, Michel (de) P : *92*

Morand, Paul P : *224*

Moreau, Jeanne P : *92*

Morgans H : *84*

Morinerie, Faïence J.B. (de la) D : *60*

Musée Carnavalet L : *78* • *80*

Musée d'Art moderne L : *90* • *118* • *146* • *166* • *182*

Musée d'Orsay L : *214*

Musée de l'Érotisme L : *234*

Musée de l'Homme L : *90* • *174* • *182*

Musée de l'Orangerie L : *62* • *128*

Musée de la Marine L : *174*

Musée des Arts décoratifs L : *62* • *90* • *128*

Musée du Grand Palais L : *138*

Musée du Louvre L : *62* • *128*

Musée du Petit Palais L : *138*

Musée Baccarat L : *118*

Musée Grévin L : *14*

Musée national des Arts asiatiques-Guimet L : *118* • *182*

Musée Picasso L : *78* • *80*

Musée Rodin L : *214*

Musée Victor-Hugo L : *80*

Muti, Ornella P : *56*

Nain bleu S : *70*

Napoléon P : *64*

Niarchos, Stavros P : *92*

Nicholson, Jack P : *214*

Niro (de), Robert P : *188*

Nobu R : *146*

Noiret, Philippe P : *142*

Nureyev, Rudolph P : *190*

Nuel, Jean-Philippe D : *202* • *207*

O'Poivrier R : *178*

Obélisque R : *128*

Ormes R : *182*

Osteria R : *78* • *80*

Onward S : *192*

Opalis S : 138

Opéra comique L : 14

Pacaud, Bernard C : 78 • 80

Palais de Chaillot L : 90

Palais de la Découverte L : 102 • 138

Palais Galliera L : 90

Palais Garnier L : 70

Palazzo R : 42 • 52

Palette R : 206

Parillaud, Anne P : 175

Paradis, Vanessa P : 16

Paris R : 214

Paschke, Ed P : 13

Passard, Alain C : 214

Patrick Cox S : 206

Patyka S : 52

Paul Smith S : 214

Pennac, Daniel P : 148

Per Bacco R : 234

Petit Saint-Pourçain R : 192

Petit Vendôme R : 32

Pharmacy Swann S : 42

Piaf, Édith P : 230

Pichet R : 90

Pierre Hermé S : 206 • 222

Plaza Athénée H : 118

Plein Sud S : 52

Pluvinel R : 62

Poilâne S : 214 • 222

Point à la ligne S : 174

Polanski, Roman P : 142

Prada S : 90 • 102 • 146

Prince of Wales P : 36

Prince Jardinier S : 52 • 62

Printemps S : 70 • 156

Pritzker, Jay D : 12

Proust, Marcel P : 42

Prunier R : 166

Putman, Andrée D : 84 • 89 • 91• 172 •
173 • 175

Queen Margot P : 190

Queen of Thaland P : 25

Red Hot Chili Peppers P : 142

Relais Plaza R : 90 • 92 • 102 • 103 • 166

Renard, Jules P : 82

Renoir P : 230

Repaire de Cartouche R : 80

Resnais, Alain P : 56

Restaurant du Palais-Royal R : 52 • 70

Richelieu P : 74

Ritz H : 84

Robert Clergerie S : 214

Roberts, Julia P : 214

Robuchon, Joël C : 174 • 182 • 222

Rochon, Pierre-Yves D : 8

Rockefeller, John D. P : 92

Rodolphe D : 14

Rodolphe Ménudier S : 128

Rogosky, Moritz D : 80

Rolling Stones P : 188 • 219

Rossellini, Roberto P : 161

Rossetti S : 206

Rostropovitch P : 142

Rousselot D : 160

Rykiel, Sonia D : 192

Sabbia Rosa S : 214

Sakamoto, Ruyichi P : 200

Santa Maria Novella S : 198

Schlöndorff, Volker P : 56

Schmitt, Éric D : 180

Schneider, Romy P : 56 • 161

Schuhl, Jean-Jacques P : 216 • 219

Ségalen, Anne P : 44

Seize au seize R : 174 • 182

Senderens, Alain C : 70 • 128

Senso R : 90 • 145 • 146

Sergio Rossi S : 206

Shah of Iran P : 36

Shine S : 80

Shiseido S : 52 • 62

Shozan R : 146

Shu Uemura S : 192

Signoret, Simone P : 56

Soleil R : 234

Sormani R : 174 • 182

Spears (général) P : 51

Spoon R : 90 • 146

Starck, Philippe D : 50 • 200

Stella Maris R : 90

Stéphane Kélian S : 206

Stern, Isaac P : 142

Stresa R : 146

Taillevent R : 110 • 118 • 156 • 166

Taittinger, Jean P : 126

Tallibert, Roger D : 178

Tauber, Léonard P : 159

Tautou, Audrey P : 22

Taylor, Elizabeth P : 188

Tcherny P : 211

Théâtre de Chaillot L : 174

Théâtre des Champs-Élysées L : 102 •
118 • 146 • 166

Théâtre des Deux Ânes L : 234

Théâtre du Palais-Royal L : 14

Thiers, Mme P : 168

Tiffany's S : 14

Toulouse-Lautrec P : 230

Tournesol R : 166

Tracy, Spencer P : 161

Trintignant, Jean-Louis P : 56

Troisgros, Michel C : 138

Tuttle, Ed D : 12

Ty Coz R : 156

Van Cleef & Arpels S : 66

Vanderbilt, Cornelius P : 92

Vanessa Bruno S : 192

Vanina Vesperini S : 214

Velly R : 156

Vendroux, Yvonne P : 212

Ventura, Lino P : 142

Versace S : 110

Versini, Dominique C : 156

Vianello, Toni C : 78

Villa Beaumarchais H : 46

Villa Lutèce H : 46

Villa Royale H : 46

Villaret R : 80

Vin sur vin R : 214

Violon d'Ingres R : 214

Voltaire P : 180

Voltaire R : 206

Vongerichten, Jean-Georges C : 146

Vuitton S : 90 • 102 • 192

Welles, Orson P : 142

Westbrook, Robin D : 186

WH Smith S : 42 • 62

Wilde, Oscar P : 4 • 186 • 188

Wilder, Gene P : 142

Willi, Anne D : 80

Wilson, Lambert P : 56

Wolf, Émile P : 131

Women Secret S : 182

Yves Saint Laurent S : 42 • 110 • 166 • 174

Yoshino, Tateru C : 90

Zagorski S : 206

Zara S : 70 • 174

Ze Kitchen Gallery R : 198

Zebra Square R : 178 • 180 • 182

Photo credits:

All photographs are by Daniel Aron: © Daniel Aron.

From the same publisher and author:

Provence of Alain Ducasse, 2000

52 Weekends in Europe, 1999

From the same author:

Paris Vins, éditions du May, 1987

Guide des stations de sports d'hiver, Julliard, 1995

Paris Fines Gueules, 1996, 1997, 1998, 2000

Chairs de poule, Noésis, 2000

Recette pour une cocotte, Staub, with Kaori Endo, 2001

Miam miaou, recettes pour chats modernes, Noésis, 2001

Comment se faire passer pour un critique gastronomique sans rien y connaître,

Albin Michel, 2002

Contributor to:

Guide GaultMillau 1981, 1982, 1983, 1984

Vins et Vignobles de France, Larousse, 1988

Zagat Guide Paris, 1999, 2000, 2001, 2002, 2003

Voyages d'écrivains, L.F. Céline in New York, Plon-Le Figaro, 2002

The author wishes to thank:

Eve Baume, Danièle Bertolino, Augustin Benetti, Françoise Boucher, Isabelle Cadd, Florence
Chevalier, Jean-Louis Costes, Yves Dantoing, Roxane Debuisson, Patrick et Nicole Derderian,
Pamela Favre, Françoise Lavédrine, Patrick Lecuiller, Laurence Lefebvre, Grace Leo-Andrieu,
Didier Le Calvez, Vanina de Malhmann, Axelle Marois, Leah Marshall, Catherine Martel,
Pierre-Martin Roux, Isabelle Maurin, Marie-Claude Metrot, Sylvie Michel, Laure Mignot,
Marie-Florence Privé, Cédric Reversade, Anne-Charlotte Romary, Adelaïde de Rouget,
Thibault Ruffat, Carole Rodriguez, Claudia Schall, Laurence Seguin, Véronique Valcke,
Laurent Vanhoegaerden.

Warm thoughts for my angels of eternity: Kaori, Jean Malti and Lanka

Thanks to all who have entrusted me with the "keys" to the traveller's Heaven! - the photograph.

Roll on to the next!